# Still Sta



## But Never Standing Still

*A Devotional Journal*
*For Those Who Care*

(three months)

Grace Disability
Marginalised Hope
Strong
Faith NeverStandingStill Love
Elderly LearningDisability Anxiety
Fostering
StillStanding
Palliative
MentalHealth Adoption
Trauma
Dementia Illness Peace

Shoehouse Publications

Email: info@shoehousepublications.co.uk

Lifecentral Church Buildings
Little Cornbow
Halesowen
B63 3AJ



ISBN 978-1-8381555-0-6

Typeset in Minion Pro, Myriad Pro and Chapparal Pro 12/15

To Mum. Thanks for being inspiring.

* * *


# Acknowledgements

I used to imagine that books were brought into being by authors in pensive mood, gazing out to the ocean or mountains. This devotional journal was mostly written in the midst of noise and often chaos. Thanks to Team Bradshaw for pulling it all together: Adrian, for your many hours of patient editing, Jane for your wise words and constant enouragement, Sophie for taking on the challenge of illustrating for the first time and Wil for all your technical support. Thanks to Sylvia and John for proofreading and to Russ for helping wih the cover.

* * *

All those in the caring community who have embraced us and helped us see that we are not alone in navigating a massive life change.

* * *

Lifecentral - for so much, but especially for being a church that cares and lives out its mission of helping people to find and follow Jesus.

* * *

Wil and our children Sophie Grace, Faith, Sophie Rose, Adam and Luke, you are my heartbeat xx

# Introduction

I am beyond excited that you are reading this devotional journal. The world needs more people like you. Whether you sought out your caring role or it came and found you, you are the heroes so often unsung. Everyone has seasons where life is particularly hard or challenging and we need some extra support. But for many with caring responsibilities, there isn't a definite conclusion: it is just a different way of doing life. We can be grateful for settled periods, but even in those times there is always an added dimension. I am in awe of all of you who care in whatever capacity, year in, year out, often with far less support than you need. We can wonder if we are getting it right, and, in some circumstances, it can take a long time before we see any positives.

The caring role can be so many things: joyful, rewarding, challenging, exhausting and isolating to name a few! We are often battling for, and even sometimes with, those we care for. There are growing numbers of people of all ages in our communities who are in need of support, with people living longer and resources being overstretched. But for each one who needs some form of care, my hope is that there will be at least one person who will be there for them, and ensure that their needs are being met.

In writing this devotional, I wanted to remind you that even if things are tough, you are not alone and there is hope. I thank God for each of you and pray that you will find encouragement, comfort and inspiration to stay standing and live well, through every season. As you take time each day to connect with God and deepen your relationship with Him, you will be strengthened and renewed to face all that life is. This devotional doesn't have all the answers, and I recognise that everyone's story is unique. You will have experiences that I know nothing about, yet, in hearing other's stories, I hear familiar themes and we share some commonality.

If you are new to faith, or still working out what your beliefs are, my prayer is that you will discover the 'heights and depths' of God's love for you. In the Bible, people usually started their faith journey through hearing and responding to the message that God's followers brought. In the New Testament, some encountered Jesus Himself and it all started by having a simple but often profound conversation. As you read about prayer in these pages, if it is unfamiliar, please be reassured that it isn't anything lofty or grand. It really is just talking with God, no fancy words required. Faith is a lifelong journey that can start or grow today. We can come as we are and God promises that, when we ask, He will forgive all that we have ever done wrong and He will help us to live through His power.

There are five devotions per week, then a reflective review for Saturdays and Sundays, as I understand that weekends can be extra busy with little space for yourself. It may help to jot down specific prayers, or things that God has spoken to you about, to be able to look back and see how far you have come. Scriptures are taken from the New International Version (NIV), unless otherwise stated.

# Chapter 1
# *WISDOM*

*James Chapter 1 v 5 "If any of you lacks wisdom, you should ask God, who gives generously to all without finding fault, and it will be given to you".*

I have prayed for wisdom many times in my life and even more so since becoming a carer. I know I am not alone in sometimes feeling daunted and overwhelmed. It is a formidable task trying to care well for a person with complex issues, whilst juggling the rest of the family's needs and fighting for the right support. It can seem that whatever we give is never enough.

Hannah in the Bible was childless and prayed desperately for God to give her a son. *1 Samuel Ch 1 v 11 "And she made a vow, saying, 'Lord Almighty, if you will only look on your servant's misery and remember me, and not forget your servant but give her a son, then I will give him to the Lord for all the days of his life."*

It would have been a harsh existence at that time to be childless, but God heard Hannah's cry and Samuel was born, only for Hannah to give him back to God as a young child to serve in the temple. I cannot imagine how difficult it must have been for Hannah to fulfil her promise and hand him over, but despite her feelings, she had learnt to trust God's wisdom. If Hannah had not allowed others to care for and nurture Samuel, he wouldn't have fulfilled his God-given destiny. Almost all of those we care for will need some outside help in various ways. But even if we have fought for it, it can be the hardest thing to accept. Whether we entrust these loved ones or are trusted with them, we need God's wisdom. On the most challenging of days, when we wrestle with conflicting emotions, let's remember that they are cherished by God and ultimately belong to Him.

> Lord, it can be especially hard to entrust my loved ones back to you when I have learnt to hold tight and protect them. Please give me daily wisdom as I care.

Wisdom

*Proverbs Chapter 12 v 18 "The words of the reckless pierce like swords, but the tongue of the wise brings healing".*

I'm sure, like me, you will have met people who are clever but not wise. In the caring role, we often function under pressure on a daily basis. Add in lack of sleep and it's not difficult for other's unwise words to press all the wrong buttons. Over time we may become more assertive but there can be the temptation to be defensive and in turn, sharp or aggressive. It is never nice to hear criticism or unintended abuses, but it cuts even deeper when we are giving everything we have and battling to make it through the day. Responding in a Godly way in what we say is not always easy, but God will give us wisdom in this too, if we ask. People who are hurting often hurt others, and only God knows their full story.

Jesus was no stranger to being insulted and hearing hurtful words. In fact, he was also arrested, stripped naked and beaten. *1 Peter Ch 2 v 23 "When they hurled their insults at him, he did not retaliate; when he suffered, he made no threats. Instead, he entrusted himself to him who judges justly".* Jesus either spoke with wisdom, or He didn't say anything. God knows what is really in other people's hearts. He also has the final say, even when others don't recognise His authority. We too can choose to think the best of others and speak life and kindness into their lives. We can allow God to be the judge of their intentions and be released, as we hand that responsibility back to Him.

> Lord, in my caring role help me to recognise how much You value me. Help me to respond to others in the right way, even when they say the wrong things.

Wisdom

*1 Thessalonians Ch 5 v 15 "Make sure that nobody pays back wrong for wrong, but always strive to do what is good for each other and for everyone else. Don't repay wrong for wrong"*

I have come to know many carers who have a depth of understanding and empathy and my life is richer for it. The flipside of how we live is that the majority of us also become reluctant warriors from constantly fighting for support or to get appointments or results, or perhaps fending off judgement from others. Even if we are not directly involved in the day-to-day care, we are all impacted by carrying the immense responsibility to protect and ensure that our loved one is being well-cared for.

Apart from Jesus, Moses was one of the greatest leaders in the Bible and one of his attributes was meekness. *Numbers Ch 12 v 3 "Now the man Moses was very meek, more than all people who were on the face of the earth".* But even this meek man and great leader acted unwisely, when he saw the suffering of his people. *Exodus Ch 2 v 11-15 "One day, after Moses had grown up, he went out to where his own people were and watched them at their hard labour. He saw an Egyptian beating a Hebrew, one of his own people. Looking this way and that and seeing no one, he killed the Egyptian and hid him in the sand".* Moses 'lost it'. We might rarely be tempted to physically hurt somebody, but in our frustration, it can take a great amount of effort to 'do good'. However, when we do, it allows us to move forward, rather than becoming entangled in that unhealthy kind of conflict, which pulls us down.

Let's take a few moments today to think about how we respond to others and ask God to show us if there are any past hurts that are affecting us.

Lord, give me wisdom to call out wrongdoing in a Godly way, to follow your example in not repaying wrong for wrong but being gracious as You are gracious with me.

Wisdom

There is a saying that "God will only give us what we can handle". So it can become confusing if we reach the point of sinking under pressure or even burnout. But this saying is a misguided notion, often well intended, yet one that can cause discouragement. Some say it comes from way back in Bible days, from a church in a city called Corinth. The Apostle Paul wrote to remind them that we are all tempted and often do wrong things. In this, Paul encourages the church, saying *"No temptation has overtaken you except what is common to mankind. And God is faithful; He will not let you be tempted beyond what you can bear. But when you are tempted, He will also provide a way out so that you can endure it" 1 Corinthians Ch 10 v 13.* Rev Shawn Coons addresses this 'half-truth' in his blog. Here in the Bible, Paul talks specifically about temptation, but he is not speaking about the trials of life that we endure. We can choose to avoid temptation, but we may often reach the point of feeling overwhelmed with the pressure of circumstances. Before Jesus was crucified, He cried out to His father, *"My soul is overwhelmed with sorrow to the point of death" (Matthew Ch 26 v 38).*

Jesus Himself and many other strong leaders in the Bible knew what it was to be overwhelmed. Jesus invites us to come to Him, not trying to hide the mess and confusion. There may be times where He changes our circumstances, or we may grow as He strengthens us to go through them. There is wisdom too, in recognising that our own understanding has limitations. *1 Corinthians Ch 13 v 12 "For now we see through a glass, darkly; but then face to face: now I know in part; but then shall I know even as also I am known". (KJV)* Let's ask ourselves today, "What am I carrying and how am I coping?"

> Lord, give me the wisdom to recognise when I need You and help me to 'cast my cares on You'. Please encourage me and help me to see clearly, when circumstances are overwhelming.

Wisdom

## Wisdom – in asking for help Friday

*Proverbs Ch 25 v 11. "Timely advice is lovely, like golden apples in a silver basket".*

Every significant event in our lives leaves an imprint, whether positive or negative. Some experiences are transformative. About two years into my caring role, I recall a point where I knew that I would never be the same again. I know that this is common amongst those who care, the recognition that we are forever changed by being stretched beyond what we thought was possible. Some people grow, whilst others are ground down. Either way, we all have good and bad days, but there is wisdom in being open and asking for help. C. S. Lewis said, "I have learned now that while those who speak about one's miseries usually hurt, those who keep silence hurt more".

It can be a big step to be honest with ourselves and those closest to us. We sometimes let guilt or unrealistic expectations rule, and we can kid ourselves that we should be able to manage. We often forget to re-evaluate as we get older, but a decade can make a world of difference to our energy levels. If we give the appearance of coping, it is hard for others to reach out. It may be that we can't physically hand over our responsibilities but sometimes, the difference can be someone hearing us and speaking life and encouragement into our situation.

Why not reach out today, join or go back to a support group, make that phone call or, if you are able, meet up with a friend? If you are feeling strong today, offer a hand of friendship to someone else. You might just be the difference to their week.

> Lord, today please give me the strength to reach out for help. On my strong days, remind me to build up others, to reach out to them and be the difference.

Wisdom

## Weekend wisdom — Saturday

*Proverbs Ch 12 v 18 "The words of the reckless pierce like swords, but the tongue of the wise brings healing".*

Jesus was no stranger to being insulted and hearing hurtful words. He either spoke with wisdom or He didn't say anything.

*How do I respond to conflict and what do I do with hurts?*

*Would any of my circumstances benefit from some wise words either from asking God or from asking a trusted friend?*

Lord, show me how and when to speak wisely and also to learn when to be silent. Thank You.

## Weekend wisdom — Sunday

*1 Corinthians Ch 13 v 12 "For now we see through a glass, darkly, but then face to face. Now I know in part, but then I shall know, even as also I am known". (KJV)*

There is wisdom in recognising that our own understanding has limitations.

*Are you growing in wisdom and making wise decisions?*

*Is there an area of your life that appears to be dark?*
*If so, ask God to take your hand and lead you through it,*
*for as long as that takes?*

Lord, you see all things clearly. Please lead and guide me as I learn to be more like you.

Wisdom

*Romans Ch 7 v 15 "I do not understand what I do. For what I want to do I do not do, but what I hate I do".*

"Growing old is mandatory but growing up is optional" (Carroll Bryant). Looking back over my youth, I cringe at some of the things I said and did. It's perhaps a good thing that I no longer live in the area where I grew up! Over the years we hopefully mature and mellow, partly due to learning from experience and partly due to the people around us, who we can learn from. We still get it wrong, but if we are wise, we will put things right.

Plants grow and thrive when they get what they need. That usually means sunshine, water, nutrients and the right kind of soil. We are not so different. We thrive, grow wiser and make better choices in healthy environments. The way that we respond to life's circumstances is rarely determined in the moment. Sometimes, we run out of patience quickly, if we have been doing too much for too long or if there are a string of difficult events. How we cope though, will also be influenced by choosing healthy relationships and conversations, the right food, exercise and most importantly, spending time with God. *John Ch 15 v 4 "Remain in me, as I also remain in you. No branch can bear fruit by itself; it must remain in the vine. Neither can you bear fruit unless you remain in me".* How is your walk with God now? What kind of fruit are you growing?

In the same way that we can't see the roots of a plant or tree, we can cover what is going on in our roots. Unhealthy roots often become noticeable when a person makes a catastrophic decision. By making positive choices daily, we build up a healthy reserve that we can draw on when needed. It increases our capacity to manage when an unexpected crisis comes along.

Lord, help me to make wise choices to grow closer to You,
and bear fruit that will last and be a blessing to others.

Wisdom

## Wisdom – in trust

Tuesday

*Proverbs Ch 3 v 5-6 "Trust in the Lord with all your heart and lean not on your own understanding; in all your ways submit to him, and he will make your paths straight".*

This is a verse that even my children can quote (with actions)! It is easy to reel off, especially if we have never had to trust God in anything with life-changing consequences, or in the things that make no sense.

I can say, "I trust in God", but then lie awake at night worrying about what might be. C. S. Lewis said, "You never know how much you really believe anything until … it becomes a matter of life and death to you. It is easy to say you believe a rope to be strong and sound as long as you are merely using it to cord a box. But suppose you had to hang by that rope over a precipice. Wouldn't you then first discover how much you really trusted it?"

Wisdom is rooted in trusting God, and we learn to trust Him through relationship. There are no short cuts. Whether we are brand new to the Faith or have known God for decades, we can let past negative experiences affect our openness to Him. Where people have been less than trustworthy, we can put walls up instead of boundaries. Where things haven't worked out as we planned, we can doubt God's love for us because we see only a small part of a much bigger picture. God challenges us to take down the walls and let Him into every part of our lives. He is asking for us to trust Him wholly and completely, with no half measures, for ourselves and those we care for.

> Lord, today draw me closer to knowing You, so that I can learn to trust You more, both for my own life and the lives of those I carry responsibility for.

Wisdom

*James Ch 1 v 22 - 24 "Do not merely listen to the word, and so deceive yourselves. Do what it says. Anyone who listens to the word but does not do what it says is like someone who looks at his face in a mirror and, after looking at himself, goes away and immediately forgets what he looks like..."*

When my eldest daughter was a toddler, she went through a climbing phase. As rookie parents, she took us by surprise a few times with her daring feats. We once found her two thirds of the way up a ladder and promptly yelled for her to come down as we raced over to catch her if she fell. She looked bemused and asked why? Her understanding was limited, and she had no point of reference for the consequences of falling from a great height. Grown-ups must seem quite dull to children. We have to teach them everything except mischief!

Obedience seems like an old-fashioned word in today's world where it's all about our rights to fashion our own destiny. Even some Christians view obedience as God wanting us to do things that we don't want to do. But it is so much more than doing good deeds or avoiding harmful behaviours. Obedience comes out of a loving relationship. We put boundaries in place for our children, or those we care for, because we love them and want them to be safe and to thrive. God wants far more for us than knowing what the Bible says. He wants us to believe in Him and grow to be more like Him. When we are being obedient to God, we grow in intimacy with Him. It allows God to shape our lives. In Genesis 32 v 28 Jacob wrestles with God through the night. But God isn't angry with him. *"Your name will no longer be Jacob, but Israel, because you have struggled with God and with humans and have overcome"*. God wants to encourage us and help us to follow His ways.

Lord, help me to surrender to You and thank You that I can start anew each day.

Wisdom

*Ephesians Ch 4 v 32 "Be kind and compassionate to one another, forgiving each other, just as in Christ God forgave you".*

There was a time in my youth when relationships were disposable commodities. If things didn't work out, or someone hurt me, it was easy to shut them out and move on. There is a legitimate place for leaving behind toxic relationships, but I'm happy to say that I value people so much more now and recognise the wisdom in how we work through differences. When we are humble and fully allow God's wisdom into our family and friendships, He gently shows us our own areas for growth. This in turn helps us to be more gracious with others when we recognise that none of us are finished articles.

When a flatbed lorry is carrying a heavy load, it often displays warnings to other drivers to make allowances and to naviage around them with caution. As carers, we are always carrying that invisible extra load that is often unseen by those around us. Even those closest to us can't always appreciate what each of us is carrying. It is good for us to remember too that most people are dealing with issues that we know nothing about.

Let's remind ourselves that we have extra pressures and we need to adjust accordingly. We may need more kindness towards both others and ourselves. When it comes to those we love, it is a choice to think the best of their intentions and when they get it wrong to forgive and move on. *Romans Ch 15 v 5 "May the God who gives endurance and encouragement give you the same attitude of mind toward each other that Christ Jesus had".*

> Lord, thank You for accepting me with all of my faults and failures. Please give me wisdom in my relationships, to know when to speak and when to be silent, and help me to forgive.

Wisdom

*Romans Ch 12 v 2 "Don't copy the behaviour and customs of this world, but let God transform you into a new person by changing the way you think". (NLT)*

My husband and I have made a few unwise decisions in our married life. For example, he has a dust allergy and we bought a duvet made of duck down. The duvet is essentially a big bag of dust that sets off his snoring every time he turns over! We can be unwise in our thinking, but we can also easily develop unhealthy thought patterns that have a long term impact on our wellbeing.

*1 Corinthians Ch 2 v 16 "For who has known the mind of the Lord that he may instruct him?' But we have the mind of Christ".* The comedian Mark Ritchie talks about the 'tragic roundabout': a human response which many of us will relate to when conflict or fear brings thoughts that go round and round into a negative spiral. You only have to look on social media for minutes to find angst, even in the caring communities (although there is much wisdom there too). Dealing with 'the system' provides plenty of material for our minds to work with. Negative thought patterns provide a perfect environment for subtle lies to be created. We can reduce people to being only one thing and situations become much worse in our thoughts than they actually are. Jesus challenges us to change our thinking, to be wise and invite the Holy Spirit to shape our thoughts.

It takes discipline and forming new habits to change the way we think, but when we do, it inevitably changes the way we live. So how do we know if we have the mind of Christ? His signature is always love. Do we have that signature of love in our thoughts?

Lord, show me thought patterns that I need to change and prompt me to invite You in.

Wisdom

*Romans Ch 12 v 2 "Don't copy the behaviour and customs of this world, but let God transform you into a new person by changing the way you think". (NLT)*

My husband and I have made a few unwise decisions in our married life. For example, he has a dust allergy and we bought a duvet made of duck down. The duvet is essentially a big bag of dust that sets off his snoring every time he turns over! We can be unwise in our thinking, but we can also easily develop unhealthy thought patterns that have a long term impact on our wellbeing.

*1 Corinthians Ch 2 v 16 "For who has known the mind of the Lord that he may instruct him?' But we have the mind of Christ".* The comedian Mark Ritchie talks about the 'tragic roundabout': a human response which many of us will relate to when conflict or fear brings thoughts that go round and round into a negative spiral. You only have to look on social media for minutes to find angst, even in the caring communities (although there is much wisdom there too). Dealing with 'the system' provides plenty of material for our minds to work with. Negative thought patterns provide a perfect environment for subtle lies to be created. We can reduce people to being only one thing and situations become much worse in our thoughts than they actually are. Jesus challenges us to change our thinking, to be wise and invite the Holy Spirit to shape our thoughts.

It takes discipline and forming new habits to change the way we think, but when we do, it inevitably changes the way we live. So how do we know if we have the mind of Christ? His signature is always love. Do we have that signature of love in our thoughts?

Lord, show me thought patterns that I need to change
and prompt me to invite You in.

Wisdom

## Weekend wisdom — Saturday

*Romans Ch 15 v 5 "May the God who gives endurance and encouragement give you the same attitude of mind toward each other that Christ Jesus had".*

When we are humble and fully allow God's wisdom into our family and friendships, He gently shows us our own areas for growth.

*What is my attitude of mind towards others?*

*Am I as kind to myself as I am towards others?*

Lord, help me to harness your endurance, to develop an attitude of mind that reflects you.

## Weekend wisdom — Sunday

*Romans Ch 12 v 2 "Don't copy the behaviour and customs of this world, but let God transform you into a new person by changing the way you think. Then you will learn to know God's will for you, which is good and pleasing and perfect".*

Negative thought patterns create the perfect environment for subtle lies to be created.

*Do I have any thought patterns that need to be shaped by the Holy Spirit?*

*Are there any of my behaviours that need to be transformed by God, to have a signature of love?*

Dear Lord, as You work in my life, transform me and show me Your will for my life.

W i s d o m

# Chapter 2
# *Resilience*

*Psalm Ch 37 v 23-24 "The Lord makes firm the steps of the one who delights in him; though he may stumble, he will not fall, for the Lord upholds him with his hand".*

Resilience is the ability to overcome difficulties, or to keep going through tough times. Many carers seem to have it in bucket loads, and I've heard some say, "What option do we have?" We are not unaffected though, and according to the Mental Health Foundation, 71% of carers have poor physical or mental health. There are many internal and external factors that impact our ability to bounce back. Some people are able to keep going, but others become battered and bruised, or cynical in the process.

Job, in the Old Testament, showed incredible resilience, even though he lost almost everything and everyone dear to him. He had been a man of high standing and great wealth, until tragedy ravaged his family and livestock. Then Job's situation became even worse with ill health, and his wife told him to *"Curse God and die!" (Job Ch 2 v 9)*, but Job was steadfast in his faith and refused to give up. Neither did he blame God for any of his suffering, for which God later honoured him and blessed him with a great increase in family and possessions (Job Ch 42 v 12-14). Job knew and trusted his God, despite what was happening around him. I don't know how I would respond in those circumstances, but I do know that when we surrender to God, He does the deepest work when we are in the darkest or most barren places.

> Lord, thank You for your promise to catch me when I stumble. Thank You for being my source of joy even in bleak moments, and for working in my life, whatever my circumstances.

Resillience

## Through anxiety Tuesday

*Philippians Ch 4 v 6-7 "Do not be anxious about anything, but in every situation, by prayer and petition, with thanksgiving, present your requests to God. And the peace of God, which transcends all understanding, will guard your hearts and your minds in Christ Jesus".*

Several years ago, my friend asked me to go to Africa with her on behalf of the church. I had previously loved travelling but had stopped when we had children. I agreed to go, but over the following weeks, I imagined every possibly disaster that might leave my children without a mum. It seems ridiculous, but I couldn't shake the anxiety; it hung on me like an old overcoat. The trip came around and all was well in the end, though it wouldn't be the last time that I would know what it was to carry that overcoat. It is a common emotion that we all feel at certain times, in anticipation of what may happen. It comes on a spectrum, from a mild unease, right through to anxiety disorders. It is different from fear because it is based more on the unknown or the possibility of something going wrong. Sadly, anxiety is on the increase and is prevalent amongst carers – not discriminating across class or culture.

We can see many examples of strong people in the Bible who felt anxious, from shepherds to kings, so we are in good company. When Paul wrote to the church in Philippi, he wasn't saying ignore your feelings, but he encourages us to take them to Jesus, who wants to give us peace. It can take time to get into a new rhythm of bringing our worries to God, before anxiety takes hold. Paul is also telling us to reflect on what we can be thankful for, and that shifts our perspective. It may also be the time to relook at our self-care or seek professional counsel, and there is no shame in getting the help and support we need.

> Lord, thank You that when I give You my cares, you will meet me and give me peace. Please prompt me to reach out for help when I need to.

Resilience

For the majority of us, at least some of our circumstances would not be our first choice, whether in present or past events, or what we may have to face in the future. As much as we love and accept the person we care for, the various challenges that come with illness, trauma, incapacity or vulnerability can be harder to get used to. Disappointment, if left unchecked, can become a shadow that hangs over us.

The disciples knew what it was to feel disappointment, because they hadn't understood all that Jesus had said to them. On the same day that Mary found the tomb empty, two disciples were on their way to the village of Emmaus. They were deep in conversation about the events of the past days, and were consumed with sorrow and disappointment. A man asked them to tell him what had happened and, not realizing that this was Jesus Himself, they said, *"Jesus of Nazareth was a prophet, powerful in word and deed before God and all the people. The chief priests and our rulers handed him over to be sentenced to death, and they crucified him; but we had hoped he was the one who was going to redeem Israel". (Luke Ch 24 v 19-21)* Not only did the disciples not recognise Jesus, they hadn't understood what His death and resurrection meant for humankind.

We often focus on the here and now, losing sight of the bigger picture; then the weight of disappointment pulls us down. The antidote to disappointment is contentment, but there will be times when we can't find that in our circumstances. We can find contentment though, in recognising that God has a plan for our lives, and He will empower us to live it out. Knowing that His peace is greater than what we have to face gives us cause to pick ourselves up.

> Lord, there are some disappointments that I may never understand, and I entrust those to You. Please help me to look to You and not to the temporary, to find contentment.

Resilience

*Philippians 1:6: "Being confident of this, that he who began a good work in you will carry it on to completion until the day of Christ Jesus."*

We have fond memories of a young man who we cared for several years ago. He was like nobody I have met before or since. His character was larger than life, and with a bounce in his step he towered over me, at over six feet tall. He was full of fun and was the 'life and soul' of any event. But being learning-disabled and having autism meant that he struggled when things didn't quite go to plan. On one such day, I had probably missed a cue and he stormed off upstairs, where I could hear him throwing and breaking things in his bedroom. Wil cheerfully told our young daughters to get their coats on and off they went to the park. I carried on washing up until everything had gone quiet for several minutes. I approached his bedroom and as I looked inside, I could see that his wicker washing basket looked like an explosion of kindling around the room. I took a breath and we talked about what had happened. That night, after the house had fallen silent, Wil and I reflected on the day. We had appeared to each other as being completely calm and confident. In truth, Wil had gone out feeling anxious about leaving me there and I had been scared that I might end up going the way of the washing basket! We learnt a lot in those years.

When we grow in confidence as carers, we don't second-guess ourselves so much. Whether we get it right or wrong, we can learn from our mistakes and move on from them, and through this our resilience grows. I'm still often not feeling as confident as I may look but I know that I'm a 'work-in-progress'. Ultimately, we can build our confidence on our relationship with God and in the knowledge that He will never stop working in us. What an encouragement to never give up!

> Lord, thank you for promising to keep doing a good work in me, until I meet you face to face.

Resilience

*Joshua Ch 1 v 9 "Have I not commanded you? Be strong and courageous. Do not be frightened, and do not be dismayed, for the LORD your God is with you wherever you go".*

God spoke this to Joshua as he took over as leader after Moses had died. The Israelites had wandered in the wilderness for forty years, and Joshua was now in charge of leading them into the Promised Land. As a military leader, he was used to fighting battles, but he would now also have to be the spiritual leader to millions of people, and Moses was a tough act to follow. Joshua was a mighty man, but God knew that even the strong need encouragement and guidance for the battles ahead.

Many of us face incredible challenges, whether or not we were prepared for stepping into the caring role. It is so easy in these times for fear to creep in and sap our strength, that voice of fear telling us, "You're not strong enough to do this or to keep doing this". But God still says today, "Don't be afraid, be strong and, wherever you lack, come and get what you need from Me". When God gave Joshua a battle plan, it wasn't the same every time. At Jericho, they marched and blew their trumpets and eventually the walls came crashing down. For the next battle, they had to put some things right and the key to victory was faithfulness and obedience. If you need more strength today, ask God to give you a battle plan. Take some time, even if all you have is a few moments in between the mayhem. Find that inspiring song, or pray, or whatever works for you. Let's connect with God, who can give us the strength that we need. I hope that you will be encouraged today. *"He gives power to the faint, and to him who has no might he increases strength" (Isaiah Ch 40 v 29).*

Lord, thank You for encouraging me in your Word. Please strengthen me today and show me ways that I can also help to strengthen those around me.

Resillience

## Weekend resilience Saturday

*Psalm 37 v 23 – 24 "The Lord makes firm the steps of the one who delights in him; though he may stumble, he will not fall, for the Lord upholds him with His hand".*

When we surrender to God, He does the deepest work when we are in the darkest or most barren places.

*What does it mean for you to delight in God?*

*Can you see growth in your own resilience?*

Lord, help me to recognise that when I stumble, you will uphold me with your hand.

## Weekend resilience Sunday

*Joshua Ch 1 v 9 "Have I not commanded you? Be strong and courageous. Do not be frightened, and do not be dismayed, for the Lord your God is with you wherever you go."*

Many of us face incredible challenges, whether or not we were prepared for stepping into the caring role. It is so easy in those times for fear to creep in and sap our strength. That voice of fear telling us, "You're not strong enough to do this or to keep doing this. But God still says today, "Don't be afraid, be strong and wherever you lack, come and get what you need from Me".

*What does 'strong and courageous' look like in your situation?*

*What difference does it make, to know that God is with us?*

Lord, help me to look for strength in you and to listen for your voice, rather than to the voice of fear.

# Resilience

*Matthew Ch 11 v 28-30 "Come to me, all you who are weary and burdened, and I will give you rest. Take my yoke upon you and learn from me, for I am gentle and humble in heart, and you will find rest for your souls. For my yoke is easy and my burden is light".*

Those with caring responsibilities cannot always physically rest when they need to, and some of us are the worst at looking after ourselves, even if the opportunity does arise. Over time, it can begin to feel counterintuitive to have fun and recharge our batteries. Some days when I'm drained, I can't drive or park well. I seem to lose spatial awareness. When my teenage daughter was younger, she said, "Mummy, is the church raising building funds because of when you crashed into it"? Physical rest is vital for healthy minds and bodies but, thankfully for us, there are also other kinds of rest.

In the verses in Matthew, Jesus speaks to those who are trying to earn God's love and approval by religiously following every law from the time of Moses. This included not only 365 things not to do but also 250 commandments to follow. These people were understandably failing miserably, and feeling exhausted in the process. Jesus told them to bring their burdens to Him. He asks nothing more than that we come to Him as we are and learn from Him. In Him, we can rest from striving to please others or to be perfect. We live our best lives out of a loving relationship, where we want to imitate the God who gave up everything for us. It is then that we can receive rest and find the energy and determination to continue on the challenging journey we are on.

> Lord, please show me if there are any ways that I have missed where I could rest more. Thank You for loving and accepting me and showing me how to be more like You.

Resilience

*Luke Ch 18 v 1-7... "In a certain town there was a judge who neither feared God nor cared what people thought. And there was a widow in that town who kept coming to him with the plea, 'Grant me justice against my adversary.' For some time, he refused. But finally, he said to himself, 'Even though I don't fear God or care what people think, yet because this widow keeps bothering me, I will see that she gets justice, so that she won't eventually come and attack me!'" And the Lord said, "Listen to what the unjust judge says. And will not God bring about justice for his chosen ones, who cry out to him...?"*

The 'persistent widow' is a woman I would like to meet. I love her tenacity and that the judge was scared of her. I see this trait often in carers, who will not stop until their loved one has been provided for. It can be difficult then to understand why the God who loves us often doesn't seem to answer (or not in the way that we want Him to). Going back to my childhood, there were times when I asked God for things and absolutely believed He would answer, only to be disappointed by His seemingly stony silence. In hindsight, I can see that I was far more concerned with what He could do for me than who He is. As I get older, prayer is becoming more about how I live. It's a subtle change in posture, more about friendship than what's in it for me. Henri Nouwen says, "You must be patient...until your hands are completely open". We change in the process, as we wait on God.

There are many times in the Bible where people asked something of God, and He helped them in the moment. I have seen and believe that those 'moments' happen. But when that isn't our experience, we press on, we keep asking, we keep praying and we learn through that to hear God's heart. And this is why Jesus tells us, *"...I have called you friends, for everything that I learned from my Father I have made known to you" (John 15:15).*

Lord, help me to be patient without losing heart.

Resillience

*Psalm Ch 30 v 5 "His anger lasts only a moment, His goodness for a lifetime. Tears may flow in the night, but joy comes in the morning".*

It is important to understand joy, especially if you are in a season where happiness is in short supply. Theopedia describes joy as "a state of mind and an orientation of the heart. It is a settled state of contentment, confidence and hope". This is different from happiness, which is a transient feeling, that comes and goes, often depending on mood and circumstances. We all experience happiness and sadness, but real joy is rooted in God. It is a hope that, whatever we are experiencing now, one day all will be made new.

*Psalm 103 verse 2 "Bless the LORD, O my soul, and forget none of His benefits".* I can remember as a child singing an old hymn, written by Johnson Oatman Jr., "Count your blessings, name them one by one; Count your blessings, see what God has done...And it will surprise you what the Lord has done". Unless we intentionally remember God's goodness and the many blessings that we have experienced, the human tendency is to forget, especially when the going gets tough.

We know the familiar saying such as 'it's sod's law' or 'what can go wrong usually does'. These are mostly said in jest, but it is common when life is difficult to fall into the mind-set of 'its always me and it won't get better'. If we allow ourselves to drift into these thought patterns, it can dampen our joy and hinder the building of resilience. I've met some carers who are stretched daily beyond what should be possible to manage, and yet they search for and find moments of joy. They are not pretending that their situation is easy, but refusing to be defined only by hardship.

> Lord, thank You for real joy. Help me to remember what I can be grateful for today.

Resillience

*Matthew Ch 12 v 20 "A bruised reed he will not break, and a smouldering wick he will not snuff out, till he has brought justice through to victory".*

Very few of us will live through the caring experience without acquiring some battle wounds, and it is not always instinctive to be vulnerable with God during those times. This is especially so if we or our loved one has been wronged or let down, when we were already feeling vulnerable. Our view of God also contributes to how we respond in times of hurt. Many of us can accept the image of God as being mighty and powerful. He created the universe by uttering the words; He powerfully drove back the sea for Moses to cross on dry ground; and His Holy Spirit came "sounding like the blowing of a violent wind". When we are feeling bruised and as though our 'fire' is barely a flicker, it can be harder to accept or trust that God is also a gentle Father and wants to nurture us back.

Sam Allberry says, "Gentleness is not the absence of strength, but the application of strength to a tender situation". God is just and He notices when we experience the fallout of living in a broken world. But, in His gentleness, He wants to draw us to Himself, comfort us and heal the bruises. We have a choice though, of whether to accept the invitation. *Matthew Ch 23 v 37 "O Jerusalem, Jerusalem...How often would I have gathered your children together as a hen gathers her brood under her wings, and you were not willing!"* It can be easy over time to start to believe that bad things happen because God doesn't care. This is the opposite of the truth, but most of us drift into that mindset at various points in our lives.

> Lord, show me today Your gentleness as I open up to You again, and draw me closer to experience Your healing love.

# Resillience

*Isaiah Ch. 61 v 3 "...He will give a crown of beauty for ashes, a joyous blessing instead of mourning, festive praise instead of despair. In their righteousness, they will be like great oaks that the LORD has planted for his own glory". (NLT)*

For those who feel broken, or on the way to being so, I would not dare to be flippant about these life-changing experiences. Life may never look the same again, and it isn't an experience that can be just shaken off. But there is still hope. God is by nature a creator; we don't have to look far to see His handiwork around us. *Colossians Ch 1 v 16 "For in him all things were created: things in heaven and on earth, visible and invisible, whether thrones or powers or rulers or authorities; all things have been created through him and for Him".*

In the same way that God created the universe, billions of galaxies and trillions of stars, He wants to creatively work in us. God restores, but sometimes it doesn't look exactly as it was or even as we imagined. He is able to create a masterpiece from something that others may discard. We cannot contain God's ideas in our human thinking. I love mosaic art. It appeals to me because something beautiful can appear out of old broken tiles or crockery. What most of us would throw out, another person sees immense potential in. God always sees the potential to create something stunning out of our brokenness.

In the Old Testament, people would put ash on their heads if they were sorry for something they had done, were mourning, or in deep distress. Here in Isaiah, God promises to exchange this for "a crown of beauty". Often, we know God is at work when we somehow carry on and grow stronger, long after we have come to the end of our human capacity.

> Lord, thank You for never giving up on me and for always seeing my potential. Help me to see more of the beautiful work You are doing in me.

# Resilience

## Weekend resilience Saturday

*Psalm 30 v 5 "His anger lasts only a moment, His goodness for a lifetime. Tears may flow in the night, but Joy comes in the morning".*

Unless we intentionally remember God's goodness and the many blessings that we have experienced, the human tendency is to forget, especially when the going gets tough.

*In what ways can you recognise God's goodness in your life?*

*Have you wrongly believed God is angry with you?*
*What would it take for you to give that to Him?*

Let's pray for all those who are experiencing the 'tears of the night time' right now. If that is you, know that others are praying for you today.

## Weekend resilience Sunday

*Matthew Ch 12 v 20 "A bruised reed he will not break, and a smouldering wick he will not snuff out, till he has brought justice through to victory".*

Sam Allberry says, "Gentleness is not the absence of strength, but the application of strength to a tender situation". God is just, and He notices when we experience the fallout of living in a broken world. But, in His gentleness, He wants to draw us to Himself, comfort us and heal the bruises. We have a choice though, of whether to accept the invitation.

*Is there anything hindering you coming close to God today?*

*How might God's victory look different from ours?*

Lord, let me know your presence, drawing me close and building me up today.

# Resilience

# Chapter 3
# *Love*

*Ephesians Ch 3 v 17-19 "I pray that Christ may dwell in your hearts through faith. And I pray that you, being rooted and established in love, may have power...to grasp how wide and long and high and deep is the love of Christ, and to know this love that surpasses knowledge...".*

We cannot begin to grasp the vastness of God's love for us until we take the leap of faith and ask Him to come and live in our lives. There is nothing on earth that even comes close for comparison. The Bible explains that the revelation of God's love comes from the Father, through His Son Jesus and by the Holy Spirit (Ephesians 2:18). It is supernatural to grasp what Jesus took upon Himself on the cross because of His love for us. In that moment, He carried the weight of all wrong, sickness and sadness that has ever been and ever will be.

If you are not sure where you stand with God, perhaps today you could take that step and ask Him to live in you. Don't wait until you feel good enough because none of us will ever get there. Bring your past, your failures and fears and hand them over to Him. God will meet with you with love, forgiveness and healing. If you've made that commitment but grown cold or drifted away, take that step back towards Him today. For those of us who have known God for many years, we can go through the motions as easily as brushing our teeth. But when was the last time that the knowledge of the love of God took your breath away? Let's not accept that as just dim or distant memories.

> Lord, thank You for loving me, even when I am unlovely. Meet with me today and give me a fresh revelation of the depths of Your love.

*1 John Ch 4 v 19. "We love because He first loved us".*

Watchman Nee said, "The nature of God's love is unchangeable. Ours alternates all too readily. If it is our habit to love God with our own affection, we shall turn cold towards Him whenever we are unhappy". I think this applies to our human relationships too.

If you have grown up in a Christian family and heard about God's love for many years, it can become a mantra, but over time overfamiliarity can creep in, causing it to become a bland notion. The same can be said about loving others. We can become choosy about who is deserving, and it takes effort to connect with those who are different from ourselves, or who are not so easy to get along with. Caring for a child with both learning disability and trauma has stretched me beyond anything I had previously known. I remember going to see the band Foreigner, who sing "I want to know what love is". The realisation dawned on me that my love needed to grow massively, to meet the needs of this little person, who had turned our lives upside down. Despite lots of encouragement from friends and family, in my own strength I knew I wasn't 'cutting it'. At the concert, nowhere near a church, I sang that song as a prayer. I'm not aware that anything changed in that moment, other than, that it was the start of an openness on my part to let God begin a new work in me. That work is ongoing and it's only looking back that I can see my capacity is growing and there are steps of progress.

It can be so depleting at times if those we love and care for are just not able to give much – or even anything – back. Many carers develop an admiral aptitude for love, but we are human, and God wants to increase our love for others, out of the reservoir of His love.

> Lord, give me a fresh revelation of the vastness of Your love. Help me to love others, even when it's tough.

*Mark Ch 12 v 31 "You shall love your neighbour as yourself. There is no other commandment greater than these". (ESV)*

The measure of how we love others is impacted by the love and acceptance we afford ourselves. And our self-perception is influenced by how we think our significant others love and value us. Perhaps our views were formed in childhood, or more recently.

We may think that some people love themselves too much, but Rabbi Alan Lurie argues that "most of us don't love ourselves nearly well enough, and this is the cause of so much of the pain that is inflicted on others". He goes on to explain that, when we are infants, we are driven by survival instincts, those innate attachment behaviours, which seek affirmation from care-givers, "out of the fear of rejection and abandonment". Sometimes some of these insecurities are carried into adult life, and we mistake these feelings for love.

But real love reflects God's character. It is not fleeting or based on our insecurities. When we are honest with ourselves about who we are, with our strengths and flaws, we can accept and love ourselves and commit to growth. Rabbi Alan goes on to say:

> "...the more you truly love yourself, the less time and energy is spent thinking about yourself because you do not seek approval, try to impress, or wonder how you appear".

> Lord, help me to see myself the way that You see me, so that I can love and accept myself and be free to serve You and others.

*1 Peter Ch 4 v 8-10 "Above all, keep loving one another earnestly... Show hospitality to one another without grumbling. As each has received a gift, use it to serve one another...".*

When I think about outstanding friendship memories, my first thoughts go to the highs and lows. The time when my friend and I laughed so hard that my cream cake exploded across my face, or the time I cried in my friend's arms, after our dearly loved mentor and friend passed away. As I ponder further, memories flood back of those who I've served with, whether through work, church, or mission trips. There are special bonds that form when we help each other, and when we serve others together. Sometimes, it is uncomfortable to reach out to others because it involves taking risks. We wonder how our actions will be viewed, or, if offered, our help will be accepted. We can doubt our abilities and be tempted to stay within our comfortable spaces. Here in this scripture, Peter stresses the importance of loving and serving each other by saying "above all".

In the Bible, Luke tells a story (Ch 5 v 17 onwards) of a man who was not able to move his body. His friends wanted him to see Jesus, but they couldn't get through the crowd. The man's friends carried him, made a hole in the roof where Jesus was, and lowered him down. Jesus commended them as they put their faith into action.

I am grateful for friends who have 'carried' us through difficult times. Often it has been in the fairly mundane, doing daily life together. It may not be grand gestures, it might be baking a cake or offering a lift. God has given you gifts, according to His grace, to be used to bless other people. It might be faithfulness, that you keep showing up, through thick and thin. Maybe it's listening and being interested, a rare gift in our fast-paced culture. Take some time today to think about what God has given you to bless others.

*2 Corinthians Ch 6 v 11-13 "We have spoken freely to you, Corinthians; our heart is wide open. You are not restricted by us, but you are restricted in your own affections. In return (I speak as to children) widen your hearts also". (ESV)*

For some, our circumstances can be isolating and it's not always easy to have the face-to-face contact we need. God understands that. Out of all the people in the Bible, Jesus could have legitimately claimed not to have the time and energy for developing friendships. He knew His time on earth was short, and He had a great deal to accomplish. On paper, it would have been far more time-effective to have gathered more great-quality leaders and train them up to be evangelists. But Jesus chose a smaller group and poured His life into them. It cost Him at times. Peter denied Him, Judas betrayed Him and all of them at some point misunderstood Him. But Jesus prioritised companionship, and we should too. In the verse above, Paul speaks with great emotion and affection. He had come to know and love the people of Corinth as though they were family, but they needed reminding to stay open.

A woman once said to me,"I didn't want friends when my child was diagnosed". I was a little taken aback by her words, but I also recognised the temptation to close off from others and retreat to safety. As Karen Young says,

> "Vulnerability is the driving force of connection. It's brave. It's tender...but we've turned it into a weakness. We've made ourselves 'strong'. We've toughened up...and protected ourselves from being hurt...Here's the problem. When we close down our vulnerability, we are shielded from hurt, but we are also shielded from love...and connection. They come to us through the same door. When we close it to one, we close it to all".

> Lord, please bring opportunities for me to build healthy connections with others.

## Weekend love Saturday

*John Ch 4 v 19. "We love because He first loved us".*

Watchman Nee said, "The nature of God's love is unchangeable. Ours alternates all too readily. If it is our habit to love God with our own affection, we shall turn cold towards Him whenever we are unhappy". I think this applies to our human relationships too.

*How does the knowledge and experience of God's love increase my own capacity to love?*

*In what ways can my feelings be unreliable?*

Lord, thank you for your unchangeable, steadfast love for me. Teach me to love like you do.

## Weekend love Sunday

*1 Peter Ch 4 v 8-10 "Above all, keep loving one another earnestly... Show hospitality to one another without grumbling. As each has received a gift, use it to serve one another...".*

God has given you gifts, according to His grace, to be used to bless other people. It might be faithfulness, that you keep showing up, through thick and thin. Maybe it's listening and being interested, a rare gift in our fast-paced culture.

*How do you know if God has gifted you with a particular characteristic?*

*In what ways can you cultivate your gifts to help them to grow?*

Lord, thank you for giving me gifts to be a blessing. Please remind me today of anything that you have given me, which I have not used or have forgotten about.

*Psalm 138 v 8 "The Lord will fulfil his purpose for me; your steadfast love, O Lord, endures forever. Do not forsake the work of your hands". (ESV)*

According to Counterpoint Research, around 15% of new cars sold in 2030 will be fully autonomous. I have mixed feelings about that, but some days I know I am running on automatic. I get most things done, but I am disconnected from why I'm doing it. My family notice, I can see eyes roll as I ask the same question, because I wasn't listening to the answer the first time around. Our calling is to love and care for those we have been entrusted with, but it often involves the mundane. We can lose sight of the purpose: to create an environment where they know they are loved and they are able to be all that they can be. The many tasks are only a means to an end. The purpose is investing in the person. Mother Teresa said, "It is not how much you do, but how much love you put in the doing".

In our labours, God is also fulfilling His purpose in us. In John Gill's commentary, he explains that the work that God has started in us is yet imperfect, but is gradually carried on; God has promised to complete it and He is faithful.

> "But beware of this about callings: they may not lead us where we intended to go or even where we want to go. If we choose to follow, we may have to be willing to let go of the life we already planned and accept whatever is waiting for us. And if the calling is true, though we may not have gone where we intended, we will surely end up where we need to be" — Steve Goodier.

Maybe we need to be reminded today of the value of what we are doing.

> Lord, inspire me to keep sight of my calling. Thank You that as I work, You too are working in my life.

*1 John Ch 4 v 19 "We love because he first loved us".*

There are times when our care seems to be one-way giving, whether for now or indefinitely. Whilst there aren't always 'happy ever afters', and we may not see the benefits, something powerful is always happening in that exchange. I have heard lots of stories over the years of situations where it seemed that the care offered was having little effect, only to find out years later that the person was impacted in a life-changing way; but we may never know. If we are able to love patiently, either the situation changes over time, or we change, or both. *Galatians Ch 6 v 9 "Let us not become weary in doing good, for at the proper time we will reap a harvest if we do not give up".* "Isn't it funny how day by day nothing changes, but when you look back, everything is different..". C. S. Lewis.

In Galatians Ch 5 v 22, the Bible describes patience as a fruit of the Holy Spirit. Although some will develop patience as they mature, most of us need a work of God in our lives. Whether this is for enduring patience or kind-hearted patience, both make us more like Christ. God wants us to be fruitful and He will work in our lives when we invite Him.

Part of being able to love patiently is about acceptance. It often requires a brave step to begin to fully accept that the person we are caring for may not ever be who or what we would hope them to be. Many carers grieve over and over as milestones are delayed or missed, or the person we once knew is not the same as they used to be. But as we patiently journey towards acceptance, we open a door to being able to see new and perhaps unexpected things to celebrate.

Lord, please show me what it means to have patience, as You are patient with me. Help me especially when faced with situations that are beyond my control or understanding.

In the Bible, God asked Gideon to lead the fight against the mighty army of Midianites. Gideon was the youngest son, which in those times meant the least significant. He was also from a poor family, in the weakest clan. He had no illusions about his status. But he finally accepted his calling after putting tests before God. So, he gathered 22,000 men to fight the battle. Then comes the curveball when God says *"You have too large an army with you. I can't turn Midian over to them like this, they'll take all the credit, saying, 'I did it all myself,' and forget about me". (Judges Ch 7 v 2) (MSG).* So eventually Gideon whittles the army down to just 300 men. The odds were ridiculous at hundreds to one. You probably know that the enemy was thrown into chaos and Gideon and his ragtag army won the battle, but, through the victory, God pointed people to Himself.

I don't know how Gideon felt squaring up to an army, but I do know what it's like to feel not up to it. It takes bravery to keep loving through times of fatigue and weakness. Some caring situations do break down, no matter how much we give, and if that happens, we need to give it over to God. But when we know that God is calling us to love those who are vulnerable (with all that this entails), that is a love worth fighting for.

> "Those who overcome great challenges will be changed, and often in unexpected ways. For our struggles enter our lives as unwelcome guests, but they bring valuable gifts. And once the pain subsides, the gifts remain. These gifts are life's true treasures, bought at great price, but cannot be acquired in any other way". — Steve Goodier

> Lord, at times the odds seem to be stacked against me. Give me strength to carry on, as I remember that the victory was never mine to claim.

*Revelation Ch 2 v 2-4 "...I have seen your hard work and your patient endurance. I know you don't tolerate evil people...You have patiently suffered for me without quitting. But I have this complaint against you. You don't love me or each other as you did at first". (NLT)*

The church members in Ephesus were great at many things. But, no matter how earnest we are, we tend to wander. I remember the pure joy when I first became a Christian. I wanted to learn all that I could about God. Over the years, life, loss and busyness happen and many things don't pan out how we expect. We go through seasons where God seems distant and our devotion is replaced with religious habits. We see this time and again through the Bible. God's people forget His goodness and start wandering away.

After Jesus is arrested, Peter, His close friend and disciple, is questioned about his connection to Him. Peter denies Jesus three times. After Jesus's resurrection, He asks Peter three times, do you love me? Twice Jesus uses the Greek word 'agape' (the highest form of unconditional love), but each time Peter responds with the word 'philia', a brotherly/friendship kind of love. Each time Jesus responds by calling Peter to look after His followers. Jesus is teaching Peter that his love for God will be the central most important requirement, if he is to fulfil his calling.

This love is a beautiful gift, given freely, but it cost Jesus everything. Through His love, Jesus continually calls us to remember His goodness and come back into relationship with Him. We will find all that we need to fulfil our calling, from our first love. Out of that close relationship with Him, we can draw from the well of His love.

Lord, forgive me for the times when I wander, and thank You for drawing me back home.

*Psalm 103:11-12 (ESR) "His love for his followers is as high above us as heaven is above the earth. 12 And he has taken our sins as far away from us as the east is from the west".*

There is a story in Genesis Ch 38 of a woman named Tamar. She was abused and neglected within a 'system', that should have been there to care for, provide and protect both her and her children. We are told that her first husband had angered God. Then, when he died, his brother should have taken Tamar as his wife, as was custom to ensure that her future would be secure. But he too let her down, so she was promised the younger brother by her father-in -law. Her father-in-law didn't make good his promise, once again neglecting her, until she called out his wrongdoing. Tamar took desperate action, hiding her identity and becoming pregnant by her father in law. It wasn't an ideal solution, but God saw Tamar's predicament. God not only forgave her, but He redeemed the situation. When we read on, we learn that Tamar was blessed with twins, God chose Jesus to be born through this direct blood line.

It is ironic that the majority of carers are the most loving and giving people, yet there are times when we get abused and neglected within systems there to help us and those we care for. But we are living examples of God's forgiveness and He asks us to show the same to others. Maybe we need to forgive a life-changing wrong. If we do it will spring to mind. But for most, it is a lack of care from others or words that are spoken that threaten ours or our loved one's value as a person. Maybe the person who hurts us and the person/s we care for are one and the same. It still hurts even when it's due to trauma, mental health or disability. These hurts can weigh heavy, if we hold on to them; but when we change our posture to one of forgiveness, God will empower us to follow His example. Let us choose to forgive all and He will lift that from us.

> Lord, help me to live a life of love that forgives. Thank You for your complete forgiveness.

## Weekend love Saturday

In Galatians Ch 5 v 22, the Bible describes patience as a fruit of the Holy Spirit. Although some will develop patience as they mature, most of us need a work of God in our lives. Whether this is for enduring patience or kind-hearted patience, both make us more like Christ. God wants us to be fruitful and He will work in our lives when we invite Him.

*Can you think of situations where you are much more or much less patient than usual?*

*Can you see the fruit of patience growing in your life?*

Lord, thank you that my patience has so much potential to grow when I am open to becoming more like you. Please give me the patience that I need to do all that you ask me to do.

## Weekend love Sunday

*Revelation Ch 2 v 2-4 "...I have seen your hard work and your patient endurance. I know you don't tolerate evil people...You have patiently suffered for me without quitting. But I have this complaint against you. You don't love me or each other as you did at first". (NLT)*

This love is a beautiful gift, given freely, but it cost Jesus everything. Through His love, Jesus continually calls us to remember His goodness and come back into relationship with Him. We will find all that we need to fulfil our calling, from our first love.

*Can you think of a time when love has felt like hard endurance?*

*What kinds of things put joy back into loving others?*

Lord, forgive me when I take your love for granted. Help me to remember your goodness today.

# My Story

My story began decades ago, well before I had even thought about what my future family might look like. I was 18 years old; it was six months after my dad had died, leaving my family to cope with the trauma of sudden loss. We are a big family, and at that time I was child number seven of eight. Dad had been something of an enigma to me, though I understand him more now in the context of his history. He could be comical, hardly able to get to the punchline of a good joke for laughing. He was kind too. I remember seeing tears on his face when the news showed starving children. He also seemed inexplicably to find misfortune. If there was dog poo, his foot would surely find it, and he never failed to trip over that one raised flagstone. Sadly, he knew rejection as a child, left to be raised by his eccentric grandmother, who had grown up in even harsher times. Those experiences left a shadow over him and he was unpredictable. His explosive outbursts often took us by surprise, where with no warning he could fly into a rage. Then suddenly dad was gone.

Looking back, I think we were probably still quite dazed, and yet it didn't shock me when my mum said that she was thinking about adopting a child, specifically with disability. She has always been strong, and she had brought us up whilst coping with my dad's mental health problems and ill health over the years. None of us had any close experience of disability, but her enthusiasm was contagious. I thought it would be a great thing for her to do and I went along with her to Barnardo's to make enquiries. They understandably advised her that it was too soon, and she would need to wait until a full year had passed from being widowed, and then she could apply. Mum went away, and for the next six months she ticked the days off her calendar. When she returned, the assessment process went relatively quickly, given that she was offering to take a child with complex needs, with no ongoing support. She was then matched with James, aged three.

I can clearly remember the first time I met my brother James. I had a strong feeling that I would love him and, despite my uncertainty, I did, instantly. As I walked into the room, he screamed loudly and then licked my face from bottom to top. I was only living at home for a short time, before going off to college, and I had no idea of the level of adjustment that my mum was going through. I recall James having seizures regularly and then being sleepy from the medication afterwards. He often banged his head on the floor and screamed. I only learned many years later that the screaming was fairly constant in the early days (and even months). I also learnt that his foster carer had told mum she "must be mad" to take on a child with such complex needs and a dire developmental prognosis. James is moderately to severely learning-disabled. He has cerebral palsy, autism and epilepsy. All of which came about through battery, when he was a prem baby.

There were many challenges along the way for my mum. She later remarried, but sadly her husband died of throat cancer six years later. He had been a coalman for many years, long before health and safety became so prominent. He would have been breathing in coal dust on a daily basis and he spoke only in a whisper. I had married and moved away by then, but mum somehow nursed him, whilst caring for my brother. Even back then, respite was nigh on impossible to access. Social Services did eventually let her know she could have a small amount of help, but it was too late, as her husband had already died. She carried on and got through it somehow. James is in his 30's now and is one of the happiest people I know. He loves and is much loved by all of us. My mum continues to inspire me, and she recently said she would adopt again, if she hadn't just turned 80!

My own caring journey began after I had been married for a few years and I saw a recruitment flyer for respite carers. It appealed to me, having seen the lack of support that my mum had experienced, and so my husband and I thought it would be good to support another family. We did that for a couple of years for a boy with global delay. We were so out of our depth but did our best with the limited insight that we had. His family circumstances then changed, meaning that we were not able to provide the frequency of support that they needed. We decided to take a break. I pursued a career in Social Work, and we had our own two daughters. After a decade or so I started to become frustrated with the repetitive cycles of change in the organisation, none of which seemed to have a positive impact on the people who mattered the most. I also realised that the majority of my time was spent in front of a computer and I missed the direct contact with families.

Again, I saw an advert for house parents for young people with learning disability, and so for four years we had two students at a time living in our home during term time, whilst they attended college. Most of them also had autism, and caring for them was a huge learning curve for us. Towards the end, our girls were heading towards their teens and it became less appropriate to have young men living in our home.

We decided on fostering children and around a year later were approved by our local authority. We said we would take one child or two siblings, preferably girls to fit in with our daughters. We agreed to several potential placements that didn't happen for one reason or another. We got used to waiting anxiously for promised phone calls. Then we were asked if we could take an emergency placement of three sibling's: a girl, and her twin brothers who had been born prematurely. We were about to go on holiday abroad and so said we couldn't have them immediately. Whilst we were on holiday I thought about them often and prayed for their safety, as the case was still in court. We arrived home and the following day had a call to say we may still be needed. We waited all day and then had another call to say, 'it was on' and they would arrive in one hour. We had nothing prepared. The children arrived on a Friday teatime and Wil had one hour to go to the shops before they closed. He completely filled the car with equipment. The information at that time was that the little girl was developmentally delayed, but they hoped she would catch up in a positive environment.

I can remember walking into church on the Sunday and several people greeted us, saying that we were amazing. It was surreal. I have never felt less amazing in my life. I sat through the service holding back the tears, wondering what we had done and if we would cope. The following months were a blur. The boys were very sickly and so it was a relentless cycle of cleaning up vomit and feeding the washing machine. The little girl was way behind her peers in development, but she was initially fairly happy to follow our girls around and lap up the attention. Five weeks into the placement we were starting to relax into the swing of things a little. Then the eldest twin became ill with bronchiolitis and I had to get him to hospital quickly, where he was admitted. We stayed in for six days, whilst my husband juggled running the business and caring for the other four children. We asked for a couple of nights respite for the little girl but found our experience echoing my mum's from many years before. We eventually got the all clear at hospital and whilst I was paying for my parking on the way out, Wil rang and said the other twin was 'going downhill', also with bronchiolitis. Thankfully, he didn't require a hospital stay but by now, we were all exhausted.

Over the coming months I prayed often that there would be a family who would adopt all three children together. At the same time, it was becoming apparent that the little girl's needs were more complex than we had thought, and I began to recognise significant learning disability, as well as more emerging behaviours resulting from trauma. The honeymoon period was well and truly over. The previous Social Worker had suggested that it would be difficult to find a family for all three and whilst we knew she was right, the prospect of them being separated just didn't sit right. I started to pray differently and began to wonder if we could be the 'forever family' for them. I eventually asked Wil if he would consider it and said I would leave it with him for as long as he needed to think about it. That was the longest few weeks of my life. It was an easier decision for the twins, but we were both wrestling with fear of the future for the eldest. We weren't afraid of committing to her, but we knew that with adoption, we would pretty much be left to manage on our own. A psychological assessment confirmed that it would be unlikely that she would ever leave home and live independently.

Eventually, Wil and I talked about it again and agreed that we would pursue adoption. By now we had appointed a Solicitor, due to lots of disappointments and frustrating twists and turns in the court arena, which had left us with little trust in the system. From our past experiences, we had a fair grasp of the challenges that lay ahead. It was still incredibly testing though, adjusting to parenting a child who often pushed us away, damaged things and hurt people around her; whilst being mostly charming outside of the home. The following two years were consumed with fighting for ongoing support and recognition of the little girl's needs. Then there were seemingly endless trips to court until the adoption order was granted. The whole process took over three years from when the children came to us.

Until we cared for our daughter, I had thought that we were quite patient and competent. I had no idea how stretched we would be. I can remember the first Christmas (a notoriously difficult time for those who struggle with changes to routine). My friend had called round with a big tin of chocolate brownies. I stood chatting with her in the hallway for perhaps twenty minutes until she left. It had gone quiet and I couldn't see our daughter anywhere. I looked all over the house, until the only place left was under the kitchen table. I will never forget the shock of seeing her face absolutely covered in chocolate. These were big pieces of rich brownie, the kind that whilst enjoyable, one piece was plenty. She had eaten almost the whole tin and her stomach was absolutely huge. I couldn't believe that such a small person could eat that amount. In the bathroom later, we were left in no doubt that the human body was in no way designed to consume so much! That was just the beginning of adjusting to post-trauma issues.

We have experienced such a range of interesting and challenging behaviours and our coping capacity is growing. We often get it wrong, but we are learning to recognise our limitations and also to look after ourselves much better. We are learning how to parent and re-parent, in a way that works for our daughter. I can remember a time when I thought I wouldn't blame Wil if he couldn't face coming home, and sadly we know others whose relationships have broken down. We are so grateful for our family, friends and church, who have encouraged and been close to us, including Wil's parents Adrian and Sallie. They had already done their time of caring for children and grandchildren, but came out of retirement, rolled their sleeves up and got stuck in. In return we gave them every germ, bug and virus going. Thank you.

We regularly meet others, whose home life is far more impacting than ours. It really does give perspective and our benchmarks for success have completely changed. A win is, when at the end of each day everyone is safe, and the house is still standing. There are sometimes pangs of sadness that we can't do all the things that we used to do, but we are very grateful that it has got a bit easier each year, which we know is not the case for many carers. We are also immensely grateful for the things that we get to do, just because of other people's kind support.

There were some dark times in those years, even to the point of wondering if we would get through it. There were moments when I wondered if God had given up on us and left us to get on with it. Several times I went into the utility room, shut the door and cried or even shouted at God. Just when we thought we could take no more, there were added complications, which dragged the adoption process out further and made us wonder if we might lose the children. At other times, we have had a timely word of encouragement, or family and friends have prayed for us, and we have treasured that. Adoption stories vary dramatically, with diverse circumstances. Each person makes sense of their own journey, and each family forges its own identity, as a unit.

Ours is an open adoption, with ongoing contact and we honour the birth parents in trying their best for their children.

About halfway through the process, we had visiting speakers at our church, Paul and Priscilla Reid, from Northern Ireland. Priscilla led a prayer time 'at the kings table'. A table had been laid out with fruit and snacks etc. People were invited to come and sit for a few moments, to ask God for what they needed, whilst the prayer team prayed for them. My husband and I hadn't slept well for many months, so I eventually went and sat at the table and prayed for peace in our situation. Instantly, I saw a picture in my mind of a battle scene, and I sensed God say, "You ask for peace but I'm calling you to be a fighter". I opened my eyes, looked across the table and saw another carer, who was also going through an incredibly tough time. Again, I felt God say, "who will fight for them … I'm going to give you a voice". It is strange that I didn't get the peace that I asked for in one sense, but God gave me exactly what I needed, which was to know He was there, giving me purpose. It's only now looking back that I can see how our faith has grown up, and we know God better than we did before.

And so, our journey goes on. But if I could go back and have a chat with my (slightly younger) self as we started the process of becoming carers, I would say a few things.

> Firstly, accept that there are lots of people who 'don't get it' and it isn't your responsibility to make them understand. Professionals will come and go. Some will have insight and treat you well and some will not. You will be the only one in it for the long haul; who is fighting your loved one's corner. In that, release yourself from any guilt about persistently asking departments for information or support.
>
> Whilst some people will have agendas, there are some absolutely fantastic people out there in the caring communities. Connect with those in a similar position to yourself, even if only online. Advice from experienced carers will be invaluable.
>
> Ask for help and be kind to yourself. You don't have to justify to anyone why you need to look after yourself

and perhaps others in your family. Your wellbeing and relationships may depend on it.

Stay with or get plugged into a good local church, where you can be loved and supported. Your situation may be so complicated that it takes a long time to find somewhere to be connected, but don't give up. If you struggle to get out, some churches have multiple services and flexible small groups.

Don't compare how you feel 'behind the scenes' to how other people appear in public. Judging from appearances can be wildly inaccurate. Other carers may look as though they are coping brilliantly, whilst quietly falling apart. The person who seems to be like Mary Poppins might be more like Miss Trunchbull behind closed doors or vice versa.

Allow yourself to be imperfect. Everyone has struggles and at times gets it very wrong. Giving yourself a portion of grace will help you to start again or keep going.

And finally, keep trusting in God and His timing. Some things may not make sense for a very long time, even perhaps this side of heaven. But God truly and fully understands what you are living every day. He is right there with you, in the mess, confusion, frustration and joys.

# Chapter 4
# *Journeys*

*John Ch 14 v 6 "Jesus answered, "I am the way and the truth and the life. No one comes to the Father except through me".*

Jesus has many fans, but not as many followers. There are those of all faiths (or no faith), who admire Jesus as a good man. There are also those who associate with God and the Christian faith, but you may never guess by observing their lifestyle. None of us yet fully lives up to His example. But Jesus says come follow and we'll sort the rest out as we go.

Kyle Idleman gives a great example from the Bible that separates fans and followers.

> "In John 6, where Jesus feeds the 5,000, He has this huge group of people and then, the next day, they come looking for more food and Jesus says, "Look, no more free food. I am the bread of life, and if I'm enough let's go". And the Bible says in *John 6:66, 'From that point on, many who had been travelling with Him, no longer followed Him'.* They turned and went home! In other words, there were those who were in it for the free bread and the inspirational teaching, and those who were saying Jesus is enough".

I rarely go swimming, due to feeling the cold, and because of that, getting in the pool is a sight to behold! I eventually succumb to my kids' shouts to "just get in", and there comes that point for all of us where we have to decide whether to take the plunge. If you are a follower, I wonder today if you are holding anything back. God might be prompting you to go further or deeper, to let go of the edge. When we do that, and tell God that we are willing to follow His lead, the journey becomes an adventure.

> Lord, I know there are times when I'm more like a fan than a follower. Show me if there is any part of my life where I've been holding back.

JOURNEYS

*Matthew Ch 9 v 9 "As Jesus went on from there, he saw a man named Matthew sitting at the tax collector's booth. "Follow me", he told him, and Matthew got up and followed him. While Jesus was having dinner at Matthew's house, many tax collectors and sinners came and ate with him and his disciples. When the Pharisees saw this, they asked his disciples, "Why does your teacher eat with tax collectors and sinners?"*

At that time, tax collectors were seen as the lowest of the low. They were crooked, extorting money from the Jewish people to give to the occupying enemy. Jesus wasn't put off at all by Matthew's life choices, He saw through all of it. He saw the heart of a man who needed His friendship. I love the irony in this story. Matthew was a rogue but Jesus gave him Salvation, a priceless gift that Matthew could not steal, buy or earn. And in this exchange of an old life for a new one, Matthew completely changed direction and dedicated himself to spreading the good news to others.

When we commit to Jesus, it goes far beyond living a moral life. The Spirit of God becomes alive in us and helps us to become who Jesus calls us to be. *Isaiah Ch 55 v 8-9 "For my thoughts are not your thoughts, neither are your ways my ways, declares the Lord. For as the heavens are higher than the earth, so are my ways higher than your ways and my thoughts than your thoughts". (ESV)* When we follow Him, we go in the direction that He is heading. As carers, we already reflect God's heart, because He is for the vulnerable and the marginalised. But Jesus wants us to let Him set the course of travel and navigate where our lives are going.

> Lord, I am humbled by Your example. Help me to hear Your voice and show me Your leading, towards those You want me to reach.

JOURNEYS

*Psalm 119 v 105 "Your word is a lamp to guide me and a light for my path" (GNT)*

When I was in Africa, at the end of our trip, my friend was driving us back to the airport and we had a simple map that someone had drawn for us on a scrap of paper. The directions were easy, with only one turning that we needed to take; so, we got deep into conversation. We were heading for Johannesburg, but eventually saw a sign to say we were almost in Swaziland! We had missed the turning and were hours out of our way. Panicked, but trying to remain calm, we kept going until we came across a random stranger in the middle of nowhere. After consulting with her dad in their car, she said "My father says if you follow his directions you will catch your flight". That is when I learned that my friend can drive like a rally pro! It was surreal, but we got on that plane with moments to spare. The Bible says that sometimes we may entertain angels unaware. If there was ever a time when I've wondered about this, it was then.

When people fall away from their faith, it's rarely a sudden action, but rather a slow drifting off course. It is easy to become distracted, when there are many demands competing for our time. And God's map (the Bible) doesn't show exact coordinates for the direction our lives. If our schedules revolve around others, it can be impossible to sit and read the Bible for any length of time, and if we get out of the habit, it is all the more daunting. But God knows and can speak through just a verse or two. He knows how we forget His teaching and that is why we are encouraged to stay plugged in. *Colossians Ch 3 v 16 "Remember what Christ taught, and let his words enrich your lives and make you wise; teach them to each other". (TLB)*

Lord, please prompt me when I start to go off course,
and speak to me today as I read your word.

JOURNEYS

*Psalm 26 v 1-4 "Declare me innocent, O Lord, for I have acted with integrity; I have trusted in the Lord without wavering. Put me on trial, Lord, and cross-examine me. Test my motives and my heart. For I am always aware of your unfailing love, and I have lived according to your truth...". (NLT)*

Several years ago, we took our two daughters to visit their Auntie Jane overseas. We set off heading towards the airport and about three minutes into the journey, my then five-year-old said, "Are we nearly there yet"! The rest of us groaned, but I wonder how much we actually grow out of that understanding in our walk with God. It can be so frustrating when things don't fall into place, there are obstacles in our path, or our efforts seem wasted. We all experience times when everything seems foggy and we aren't able to hear His direction. In these moments, we can lose sight of what God is wanting to do in us along the way. He is far more concerned with who we are becoming than our arriving at the end goal of achievements. Often, God slows us down to grow our character so that we can take stock, check our integrity, values or spiritual temperature. It can be confusing and we can wonder if we ever really heard from God.

It is thought that Daniel in the Bible was only a teenager when he was taken captive by King Nebuchadnezzar. But Daniel had integrity, and he 'laid out his stall' as a young man. Daniel had no issue with being educated and trained for the king's court, but he refused to eat food that had been dedicated to false gods. (Daniel Ch 1 v 8). Daniel would have no part in pagan feasts, even though taking a stand was risking his life. It was more about knowing who he worshipped than about what he ate and drank. When 'roadworks' slow us down, let us take stock of who we are. Have we made compromises, started to blend in with society's values or grown cold towards the things of God? Does He have your attention?

Lord, please help me to see more of who You want me to 'become', rather than just what can be achieved.

JOURNEYS

*Luke Ch 10 v 38 to 42 "Jesus and his disciples...came to a village where a woman named Martha opened her home to him. She had a sister called Mary, who sat at the Lord's feet listening to what he said. But Martha was distracted by all the preparations that had to be made. She came to him and asked, "Lord, don't you care that my sister has left me to do the work by myself? Tell her to help me!" "Martha, Martha", the Lord answered, "you are worried and upset about many things, but few things are needed, or indeed only one. Mary has chosen what is better, and it will not be taken away from her".*

Whilst Martha was working hard and feeling badly done to, her thoughts took on a negative edge. I can imagine her banging the pots and pans to make a point and communicate what she hadn't yet verbalised. Outwardly, she was serving, but inwardly she was seething, thinking about her 'lot'. Jesus gently shows her what is more important, namely to take time to stop, learn from Him and build ourselves up.

I wonder if you identify with Martha: worrying that all the plates will come crashing down if you take time out. It takes discipline to sit at Jesus' feet. In 1999, a good friend of ours was diagnosed with cancer and was told it was terminal. He always seemed to know what to say, but I was lost for words. So, in his last months, I did what I knew how to do. I walked their dog, prayed a lot and stayed close. One day, coming back from their house I had a sense of complete peace. I felt the Holy Spirit say, "As you sustain others, I will sustain you". It was a liberating moment and a life lesson that has stayed with me. I realised that what we give comes out of what we receive, and God gives freely. But, to allow God to sustain us and fill us up, we need to stop at times and give God the space to give us what we need to go the distance.

> Lord, I ask that as I care, You will show me how much You care for me and sustain me. Let me know Your closeness today.

JOURNEYS

## Weekend journeys — Saturday

*Psalm 119 v 105 "Your word is a lamp to guide me and a light for my path" (GNT)*

When people fall away from their faith, it's rarely a sudden action, but rather a slow drifting off course. It is easy to become distracted, when there are many demands competing for our time.

*When was the last time that you were inspired by what you read in the Bible?*

*Can you think of a time when God's word influenced the direction that you took?*

Lord, thank you for guiding me when I read the Bible. Inspire me again to read and learn your ways.

## Weekend journeys — Sunday

*Psalm 26 v 1-3 "Declare me innocent, O Lord, for I have acted with integrity; I have trusted in the Lord without wavering. Put me on trial, Lord, and cross-examine me. Test my motives and my heart. For I am always aware of your unfailing love, and I have lived according to your truth...". (NLT)*

It can be so frustrating when things don't fall into place, there are obstacles in our path, or our efforts seem wasted. We all experience times when everything seems foggy and we aren't able to hear His direction. In these moments, we can lose sight of what God is wanting to do in us along the way.

*Can you think of a time where your plans have been frustrated?*

*Did you, or do you recognise what God is doing in your life in those times?*

Lord, when things don't go to plan, remind me that you love me just as much and are still at work.

JOURNEYS

*Proverbs Ch 16 v 9 "The mind of man plans his way, But the Lord directs his steps".*

In Acts Ch 16 v 6-10, Paul and his companions are travelling to preach the gospel. The Holy Spirit prompts them not to go to Asia and later they are prevented from going to the city of Bithynia (in Turkey). Instead, Paul had a vision to go to Macedonia, which they did. We don't know exactly why Paul was diverted from going where he intended to go. He had the gifting, the call, the opportunity and he wanted to do a great thing to preach and bring people to God. All we know is that God saw a bigger picture. We read in 1 Peter Ch 1 v 1 that those places were later reached, in God's timing. Many carers expected their lives to go in a different direction, even if caring was a choice. We mostly give ourselves freely and gladly and may never speak of goals unreached, diverted plans, or unrealised vision. But perhaps we wonder if our heart's desires and purpose will ever be found.

When things don't go to plan, I've often heard people say "God must have something better for you". But 'God's better' often means our learning and growing, rather than bigger, more exciting or better paid. Most of us live out our calling amidst encouragement and disappointment, success and failure, goals achieved but also missed opportunities. There have been numerous times where a diversion absolutely has resulted in an unexpected and amazing blessing, even beyond anything that I could have imagined. But it is not a given or necessarily for this season; there are also times of discouragement and there are dreams yet to be fulfilled. To be human is to need the guidance of God, as a sheep is led by the shepherd, to know His direction and to trust His choice of destination. I don't know if you will get to where you want to be, when you want to get there. I only know that God has not forgotten.

Lord, thank you for the dreams that you put in my heart. Please teach me how to trust you more when my plans are diverted.

JOURNEYS

*Jeremiah Ch 6 v 16 This is what the Lord says: "Stop at the crossroads and look around. Ask for the old, godly way, and walk in it. Travel its path, and you will find rest for your souls. But you reply, 'No, that's not the road we want'!" (NLT)*

Some friends of mine were walking up a mountain in Ireland many years ago. Thick fog had descended, and visibility was poor. The group decided to press on, even though they couldn't see that they were even on the mountain, but for small wooden crosses that had been placed every few feet, that gave reassurance. One of my friends said later that the image of the crosses resonated with her. God rarely shows us the full picture, but just enough for us to take the next steps and stay close and dependent on Him.

For many of us, caring creates more than the usual element of uncertainty about the future. Our human instinct is to try to work out the details, so that we know what we will be dealing with. But sometimes our own intuition is not complementary to where God would lead. That is why following God is often described as the narrow way, or the lesser paths. There can be the temptation to stray or stay on expected territory, where we can find the familiar and the comfortable. But when we do walk closely with God, we can find an assurance and peace that defies logic.

As well as communicating with us through the Bible, God speaks in many ways, in circumstances, through people and in answered prayer. Even if God called you to be in a particular situation, it doesn't necessarily mean that He is calling you to stay there forever. Many years ago, a friend sent me a Bible verse and it confirmed what I had felt God was saying about the skills I needed to develop. Another person quite bluntly pointed out a vulnerability in me and it was a 'lightbulb moment', that has positively influenced my relationships. So, let us keep praying for each other and be ready to speak. We may be someone else's signpost in times of uncertainty.

> Lord, help me to stay open to Your leading and show me who I can pray for today.

JOURNEYS

*Isaiah Ch 43 v 19 "Behold, I am doing a new thing; now it springs forth, do you not perceive it? I will make a way in the wilderness and rivers in the desert". (ESV)*

In the Bible we can read the story of the Israelites. After God helped them to escape from 400 years of slavery, He promised them a land "flowing with milk and honey". Moses sent some men ahead to spy and scout out the land. Word came back that the land was full of fearsome giants (enormously tall men). Only two leaders, Joshua and Caleb, saw beyond the obstacles and believed that God would do what He said He would. God could have got them to the Promised Land by a much quicker way than through the desert, but they were not ready to take hold of their destiny. So, they wandered, and months turned into years, which turned into four decades. Whilst they wandered, God was patient and faithful, making sure that they had all that they needed.

There have been times when I have struggled with the same issues over and over again. I've had a glimpse of God's leading but have tripped over personal 'roadblocks', and have been left wondering why I wasn't able to move forwards. Also, God's leading hasn't always made sense. Like so many who care, I felt for a long time that I should be a voice for those who are not able to stand up for themselves. But I don't process information quickly and at times I used to offend with clumsy words. I would then hold back when I knew God was prompting me to speak. Sometimes, we sense God's leading but 'wander' because of self-doubt. I would not have chosen to go through the times where I got it wrong, or felt vulnerable. But through experience I have 'got over myself' and am peaceful about following God's lead. We don't always see what God is doing at the time, but He is leading and making a way.

Lord, thank You for your incredible patience and for providing for me for as long as it takes.

JOURNEYS

*Matthew Ch 17 v 1-3, "...Jesus took Peter and the brothers, James and John, and led them up a high mountain. His appearance changed from the inside out, right before their eyes. Sunlight poured from his face. His clothes were filled with light". (MSG)*

There is nothing supernatural about mountains, God is just as awesome and powerful in the valleys. But they have great significance throughout the Bible and God's glory is revealed in them time and time again. He makes a covenant with Noah on a mountain after the floods; He meets Abraham there; He gives the commandments to Moses and, on the same mountain much later, He speaks to Elijah. Before His crucifixion, Jesus came away from the crowds after teaching and spent the nights on the mount of Olives (Luke 21:37)

It is no surprise that there are many health and wellbeing benefits when we come away from the noise and pollution of the towns and cities. Higher up, the air is cleaner, and we have a vantage point both naturally and spiritually. We may not have the opportunity to get away and climb higher, but God still calls us upwards. He beckons us to live a higher calling of holiness. And not so that 'we can boast', that we are different because of anything we do in our own efforts, but because we pursue God and submit to His ways. The higher calling glorifies God because it comes from Him, and we live it through a work of the Holy Spirit.

Next time you have the opportunity, go higher and remember what God did in those places, and let all else fade into the background. Matthew Ch 17 v 8 *"When they looked up, they saw no one except Jesus".*

JOURNEYS

*Hebrews Ch 12 v 1 "Therefore, since we are surrounded by so great a cloud of witnesses, let us also lay aside every weight, and sin which clings so closely, and let us run with endurance the race that is set before us". (ESV)*

A long time ago, I briefly took up running, but soon realised it wasn't for me. My lack of spatial awareness made it a dangerous pursuit. I still recall the day that I decided to find an alternative form of exercise after falling into a ditch. My sister Sharon was not doing much cheering on; in fact, she was laughing uncontrollably at my downfall! One of my daughters on the other hand was a great runner, but she rarely won because she could never resist that sideways glance to see how everyone else was doing. It was fatal to her winning chances, as the comparison game usually is.

These verses encourage us to let go of anything that stops us from becoming more like Jesus, as it is those things that ultimately get us tangled up and become a weight that we drag around. It is in our nature to rationalise and excuse our own weaknesses. We can get so used to being held back that it almost feels more comfortable than dealing with our baggage and letting it go. God wants us to be free from it; I know that because of the value that He placed on buying our freedom. Then we are exhorted to keep going to maturity in our faith.

We are not able to choose the type of terrain that we journey through and sometimes we all wish it were a bit smoother. We cannot judge our performance on how someone else is 'running their race'. Many of us know what it is to feel judged (or worry about being so) as our circumstances often don't quite fit 'the norm'. But know that God is cheering you on.

Lord, thank You for the price You paid for me. Help me to keep going and run well.

JOURNEYS

## Weekend journeys Saturday

*Proverbs Ch 16 v 9 "The mind of man plans his way, But the Lord directs his steps".*

To be human is to need the guidance of God, as a sheep is led by the shepherd, to know His direction and to trust His choice of destination.

*What comes to mind*
*when you think about diverted plans in your life?*

*Is there anything that you believe God has put in your heart*
*that is yet to be fulfilled?*

Let's bring that to God again today and ask Him to speak to you about where He wants to lead you.

## Weekend journeys Sunday

*Isaiah Ch 43 v 19 "Behold, I am doing a new thing; now it springs forth, do you not perceive it? I will make a way in the wilderness and rivers in the desert". (ESV)*

In the Bible, we can read the story of the Israelites. After God helped them to escape from 400 years of slavery, He promised them a land "flowing with milk and honey". …Word came back that the land was full of fearsome giants (enormously tall men). Only two leaders, Joshua and Caleb, saw beyond the obstacles and believed that God would do what He said He would.

*Think back over recent years. Is there any area*
*where you sense God wants to do something new?*

*Are there any obstacles that are preventing you*
*from leaving 'the old' behind?*

Lord, help me to be open and recognise when it is time to move on.

JOURNEYS

# Chapter 5
# *Faith*

*Hebrews Ch 11 v 1 "Now faith is the assurance of things hoped for, the conviction of things not seen". (ESV)*

People generally have faith in something to a greater or lesser degree. I've only met a few who think there is nothing outside of what they experience through their senses. But having faith in God is more than a belief that He probably exists. God is looking for true disciples who will do what He asks and who will hold on to their faith whether life is good or bad. Paul tells us in Ephesians that faith is a gift, we cannot earn it, but we can look after and nurture it. It may take greater faith to believe that God is 'working for good' in ours or our loved one's lives, when we cannot yet see what He is doing.

When I became a Christian at a young age, it was straight-forward. There were no competing voices or barriers that arose from life's experiences. It was a decade or so later when I became troubled and started to question my faith. As I wrestled with doubts, a wise friend reassured me that it is healthy to go through a season of questioning to work out what we believe, aside from that which is inherited from our parents or others. As I came through that, I felt God asking me to choose maturity in my faith. I prayed and made a commitment that no matter what was shifting and changing around me, I would trust the God who never changes, and I would be all in. It didn't mean there would never be any more questions, just that I would no longer be a 'fair weather' Christian. We all have that choice to make. Then when crisis hits, the decision has already been made to dig in and work it through. Bailing out is not an option. I heard someone once say, "God has no grandchildren"; we cannot live off anyone else's faith.

Reflect on your faith today and ask God to show you if you have been holding back from committing any part of your life to God

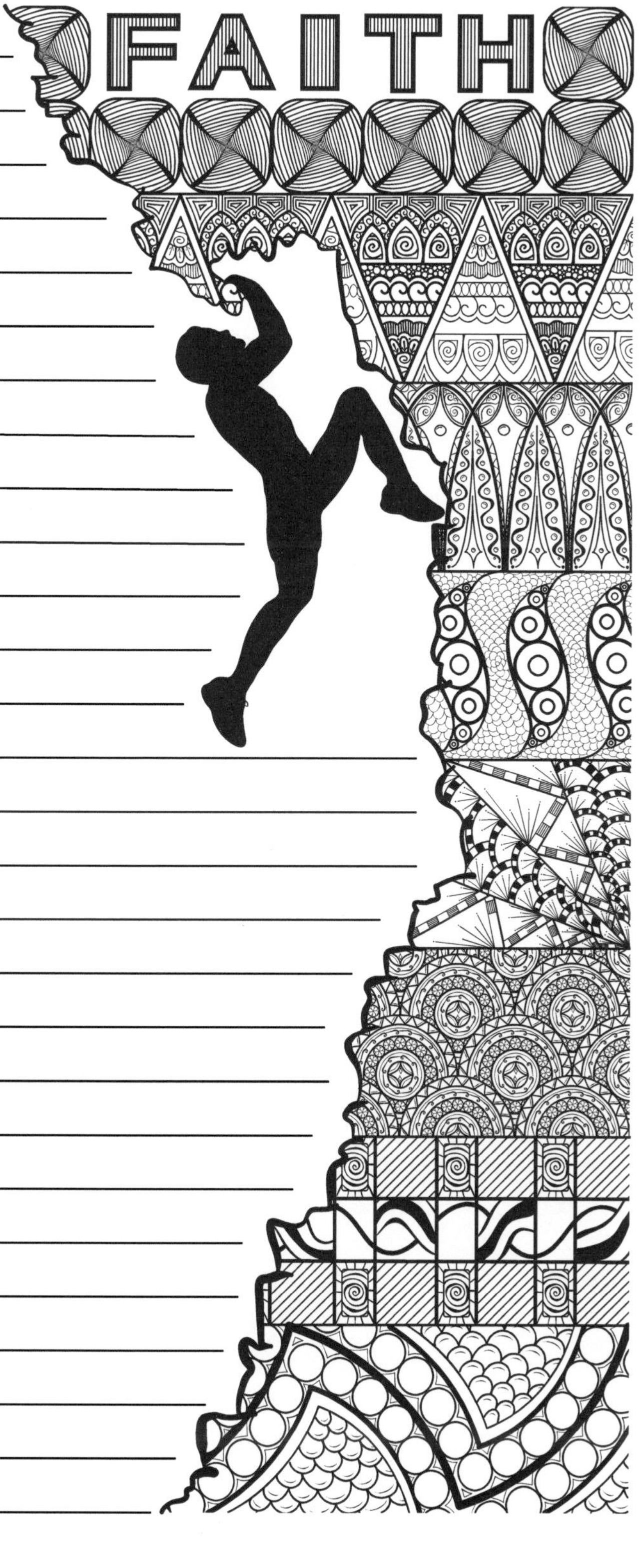
FAITH

*Matthew Ch 18 v 2-4 "He called a little child to him, and placed the child among them. And he said: 'Truly I tell you, unless you change and become like little children, you will never enter the kingdom of heaven. Therefore, whoever takes the lowly position of this child is the greatest in the kingdom of heaven'".*

When my teenagers were younger, there was a cereal promotion that involved finding a 'golden' ticket for free entry to an attraction. It was lovely to see their excitement, but we also had to help them manage expectations. As a child, I thought of faith a bit like the 'golden' ticket. I thought that if God could do great things for us, why wouldn't He? I didn't know much about the Bible beyond the stories from Sunday School. It took many years of looking at the people of faith who have gone before us to work out what it means that 'God's ways and God's thoughts are often not like ours'. We only need to look at the disciples, the men who Jesus handpicked, walked with and called His friends. Though some accounts differ, it is commonly accepted that almost all of them were martyred for their faith.

There are still groups of believers who hold extremes of faith. There are those who, long after they have grown up, still see faith as the 'golden' ticket where God will grant their desires if they just have enough faith. Then there are those who have gone through so much sadness and disappointment that their faith has an edge of cynicism.

There is a tension in having a maturing faith that doesn't lose its childlike trust. This involves believing that God 'can', whilst trusting His sovereignty when our lives or the lives of those we care for isn't what we may choose. Faith is keeping our hearts and hands open expectantly, whilst recognising that our hope is in the eternal.

Are your hands and your heart open today?

FAITH

*John Ch 13 v 4-5 Jesus washes His disciples' feet. "So, he [Jesus] got up from the meal, took off his outer clothing and wrapped a towel around his waist. After that, he poured water into a basin and began to wash his disciples' feet, drying them with the towel that was wrapped around him".*

Simon Peter was horrified that his Lord wanted to wash his feet, but Jesus said in verse 7, *"You do not realize now what I am doing, but later you will understand"*. And verse 8, *"Unless I wash you, you have no part with me"*. Jesus was teaching the disciples about servanthood, but it was much more than that. He was showing them that to be part of Him, they had to let Him attend to their needs and wash away the wrong in their lives. It took time for the disciples to see what God was teaching them and they must have felt confused at times. As carers, we can become so much more comfortable attending to others' needs, that it can feel strange to allow God to attend to ours. But when we allow God to wash away the grime that we pick up in life, it helps us to shift perspective and see fruit even in barren places.

I grow raspberries in my garden, and at the end of the season I picked what I thought was the last of the crop. The plant looked bare. I knelt and scooped up a few I had dropped. As I glanced up from underneath, I was amazed at how many I had missed. I remembered times when God has shown me that there's more fruit than we can see, if we look again from another perspective. Sometimes, we need eyes of faith to recognise what God is saying or doing; and to believe that He will bring fruit from what we have sown into others' lives and relationships. When our circumstances seem bare, we can assume that things may never change for the better. But God can produce fruit, even in barren places.

> Lord, help me to see from Your perspective and reignite faith to believe that You are doing far more than I can see. Help me to look again at situations that are perplexing right now.

FAITH

*Matthew Ch 17 v 20 "...For truly, I say to you, if you have faith like a grain of mustard seed, you will say to this mountain, 'Move from here to there,' and it will move, and nothing will be impossible for you".*

At first glance, these verses might seem a bit odd, especially if you're a literal thinker. But Jesus often used parables and pictures to make a point. These verses came after followers of Jesus had prayed for a child who was tormented, but the child hadn't been healed because of their weak faith. Jesus was frustrated with the people at that time, because they were slow in recognising that Jesus was who He said He was. But He showed compassion to the child and his family and healed him.

Barnes's commentary says that the mustard seed is the smallest of all seeds, yet it produces the largest of all herbs. Many believe that Jesus was saying that "if you have the smallest or feeblest faith that is genuine…If you have increasing, expanding…faith, growing and strengthening from small beginnings, you can do great things". Our faith may be small and even feel feeble at times, but when we pray with wisdom, according to His will, He hears us and responds. Mark Ch 9 v 24 records that the child's father said, *"I do believe, help my unbelief"*. Sometimes our feeble faith is not an afront to God, but more a reflection of battle-weariness. God knows that at times we lack what we need, and He welcomes us to come to Him honestly and ask for help. God knows our hearts. Where our faith is lacking, He supplies what we need.

Why not pray today about any 'mountains' in your life that need to be moved? Believe and ask God to help any unbelief.

FAITH

*John Ch 20 v 24-25 "Now Thomas...one of the Twelve, was not with the disciples when Jesus came. So, the other disciples told him, "We have seen the Lord!" But he said to them, "Unless I see the nail marks in his hands and put my finger where the nails were, and put my hand into his side, I will not believe".*

I feel sorry for Thomas. Apart from Judas, he's probably the least favourite disciple, being remembered for his lack of faith. But I wonder if many of us would fare better. After that first meeting, Jesus appears again a week later when Thomas is there. I'm sure Thomas's faith was already growing, as the doors were locked, and Jesus turned up, but nobody had let Him in! Jesus invites Thomas to touch His scars and then tells him to believe. Verse 29, *"Then Jesus told him, 'Because you have seen me, you have believed; blessed are those who have not seen and yet have believed'".* Thomas calls Jesus his Lord and his God and although Jesus gently reproaches him, He doesn't reject him. Thomas may have been a doubter, but he was faithful. Jesus goes on to commend those who believed just by hearing the testimony of others, and perhaps because they had recognised that Jesus was who He said He was.

It can feel natural to hide our doubts, assuming that everyone else has got their faith all sorted out. But we don't have to withdraw, if we are wrestling or going through a dry season. If our faith has taken a beating in the process of hardship, this is when we need to lean in and be open with those we trust. We can also find encouragement by remembering all that God has done in the past. David does this in *Psalm 77 v 11 "But then I recall all you have done, O LORD; I remember your wonderful deeds of long ago".*

> Lord, remind me today of the great things that You have done.

FAITH

## Weekend faith Saturday

*Hebrews Ch 11 v 1 "Now faith is the assurance of things hoped for, the conviction of things not seen". (ESV)*

Paul tells us in Ephesians that faith is a gift. We cannot earn it, but we can look after and nurture it. It may take greater faith to believe that God is 'working for good' in ours or our loved one's lives, when we cannot yet see what He is doing.

*What are you hoping for by faith today?*

*What could you do to nurture your faith?*

Lord, inspire me to nurture my faith. Lead me to search out those things that encourage me.

## Weekend faith Sunday

*Matthew Ch 17 v 20 "...For truly, I say to you, if you have faith like a grain of mustard seed, you will say to this mountain, 'Move from here to there,' and it will move, and nothing will be impossible for you".*

Barnes's commentary says that the mustard seed is the smallest of all seeds, yet it produces the largest of all herbs. Many believe that Jesus was saying that "if you have the smallest or feeblest faith that is genuine...If you have increasing, expanding...faith, growing and strengthening from small beginnings, you can do great things".

*Have you seen or experienced a miracle?*

*How did it (or how do you think it would) impact your life and faith?*

Lord, help me to believe for great things and to hold on to my faith in testing times.

FAITH

*Hebrews Ch 11 v 6 "And without faith it is impossible to please God, because anyone who comes to him must believe that he exists and that he rewards those who earnestly seek him".*

I haven't been to a gym for a long time, but I do remember it got a little easier over time. I am told that our muscles have memory and if we restart a fitness routine, it doesn't take as long to get back into shape. In the same way, faith is like muscle. If we don't keep using it, it withers and becomes weak. Throughout the Bible, God is pleased with people when they exercise faith, He responds to it and commends people for it. There are many examples of people who took risks of faith because they believed in Jesus; even when those around them would have been outraged. In Mark Ch 5 v 25-34, a woman had been bleeding for twelve years. She was considered ceremonially unclean in her culture, and forbidden to touch others. Yet she pushed through the crowd and dared to touch Jesus. After she was healed, Jesus said to her *"Daughter, your faith has healed you"*. There was also the centurion who asked Jesus to heal his servant. Again, Jesus healed the servant and said, *"I tell you; I have not found such great faith even in Israel"*. But God doesn't just look for our faith in the big things, as it says in *2 Corinthians Ch 5 v 7 "We walk by faith, not by sight"*. We need faith for our daily walk to live our lives in a way that honours God.

We can be choosy about how we exercise our faith. With fragile self-esteem, we can believe that God wants to intervene for others more than He does for me. But God wants us to take steps of faith, to pursue Him. And through that, our faith grows.

Lord, show me how to exercise my faith in You today.

FAITH

*Mark 9:23 Jesus said to him, "If you can believe, all things are possible to him who believes". (NKJV)*

I enjoy hearing evidence that supports the truth of the Bible. Aside from historical and archaeological findings, it is incredible that at least thirty-five people wrote the Old and New Testament over 1500 years with 300 messianic prophecies in the Old Testament that came to pass in the New Testament. But no amount of evidence will make faith redundant. There will always be those who dispute what the Bible says, presenting their own theories instead. Our faith is based on who and what we have not seen. We haven't yet met Jesus in the flesh, heaven doesn't do day trips and we haven't experienced living life free from ours and others' wrongdoing. The basis of our faith is in believing that Jesus was more than just a good man, a great teacher and prophet. He is the Son of God, and He came, walked amongst us, died for us and rose again.

So, when we become people of faith, we no longer live as though this is all that there is. As believers, we always have one eye on what is yet to come. We don't live just for ourselves or even for those we love and care for. We were made for more. *1 Corinthians Ch 6 v 20 "For you were bought at a price; therefore, glorify God in your body and in your spirit, which are God's". (NKJV)* As we mature in faith, we begin to recognise that living according to the Spirit is an expansion rather than a restriction. Each day has opportunities that go beyond our human vision and strength. We can ask God to show us each day, what He wants to do in and through us.

Let's not miss those opportunities today!

FAITH

*Luke Ch 21 v 1-4 "As Jesus looked up, he saw the rich putting their gifts into the temple treasury. He also saw a poor widow put in two very small copper coins. 'Truly I tell you,' he said, 'this poor widow has put in more than all the others. All these people gave their gifts out of their wealth; but she out of her poverty put in all she had...'"*

In Hebrews Ch 11, we read about many other deserving heroes of faith who started off being weak and then became strong. Those who *"conquered kingdoms, administered justice and gained what was promised"*. But this woman, who by human standards never achieved anything noteworthy, showed great faith and character and she did it without knowing that Jesus was watching her. To those around her, the widow's act was insignificant, but to God, it was greater than those who gave vast amounts. In the act of giving all that she had, she also put her life and her future in God's hands. God was moved by the widow's faithful and generous heart and for that she will never be forgotten. Jesus is far more concerned with who we are when nobody is watching us, than He is in our persona that is seen by others. We don't know the back story of this woman, but I suspect her courageous act of faith wasn't a spur of the moment decision.

We should all be generous with what God has given us, but He is not asking all of us to give away everything we have. As our faith grows out of our relationship with God, He asks all of us to be courageous as the people He has called us to be and within the circumstances that we live in. A courageous act of faith for you may be a bold life-altering gesture, or it may be something as simple as starting to pray again for someone you had given up on. It may be inviting someone to church or even just getting up to face another day.

> Lord, show me today how I can take a step in my faith in order to be courageous.

FAITH

*James Ch 2 v 14 & v 26 "What good is it, my brothers, if someone says he has faith but does not have works? ...faith by itself, if it does not have works, is dead". (ESV)*

There is no such thing as a living faith that doesn't impact our lives and influence what we spend our time doing. Nothing we could ever do will make us more or less of a Christian. But every aspect of how we live will be marked by our faith. In the book of Matthew, he tells us that others should be able to tell who Jesus's followers are *"by their fruits"*. It will be evident in the choices and sacrifices we make, the company we keep, how we treat people who think differently from us, how we care for others, how and on what we spend our money. In the same way that we would expect fruit from a healthy tree, planted in good soil, we would expect to see good fruit in the lives of those who follow Jesus. *Colossians 2 v 7 "Let your roots grow down into him, and let your lives be built on him. Then your faith will grow strong in the truth you were taught, and you will overflow with thankfulness". (NLT)*

> Don't bother to give God instructions; just report for duty
> — Corrie Ten Boom.

In Ephesians Ch 2 v 10, Paul explains that God has already prepared the good works for us to do. Unlike plants and trees, we humans don't become fruitful just by being in the right conditions and soaking up the goodness around us. Faith that works requires action. It progresses from only believing to stepping out, being obedient and sometimes taking risks. Whether we are new to the faith or a seasoned Christian, age is no barrier. Moses was eighty years old when he crossed the Red Sea, his brother Aaron was eighty-three. Joshua was eighty-five when he said to God, "Give me another mountain" (I've still got some fight in me).

> Lord, I want to have a living faith that impacts every area of my life and those I care for. Please help me to see the growth, as I learn how to build my life on you.

FAITH

*Romans Ch 1 v 12 "that is, that you and I may be mutually encouraged by each other's faith".*

When I was a teenager, my dad and some of his friends used to go around our local towns and preach on the street corners. I was mortified. They even got pelted with eggs once, which made a story for the newspaper. My dad just saw the funny side of it and wasn't deterred in the slightest. I look back now through a different lens and find myself admiring his motivation and tenacity. I wouldn't choose the method he did, which was perhaps for a bygone era, but I do agree that we have a message worth sharing.

In Paul's second letter to the Corinthian church, he tells them to examine themselves and to test their faith. When we know what condition we are in, we know if we need to do something differently. Do we have a faith that is worth sharing, both with those who don't yet know Jesus and those who know Him but need encouragement? If someone looked closely at how we live out our faith, would it be encouraging for them to see? Is our private life as godly as when we are in public? Does our faith move us to compassion for those we care for, those further afield and for those who will never give us anything back? If we use social media, do our posts lift people up or tear them down? Has criticism become easy to justify? These are important questions that act as a temperature gauge. It isn't to beat ourselves up and go looking for our shortcomings. God wants to help us to lift us up, and He instructs us to lift up others who are struggling. It is worth pausing from time to time to think about what messages our lifestyle gives to other people.

We may all have different ways to express our faith, but we should never lose sight of God's great commission to tell people about Him.

*When was the last time that you shared your faith?*

FAITH

## Weekend faith Saturday

*1 Corinthians Ch 6 v 20 "For you were bought at a price; therefore, glorify God in your body and in your spirit, which are God's". (NKJV)*

When we become people of faith, we no longer live as though this is all that there is. As believers, we always have one eye on what is yet to come. We don't live just for ourselves or even for those we love and care for. We were made for more.

*Can you think of one thing you could do*
*to glorify God in your body and spirit, through self-care?*

*What would it mean for you to have eyes of faith?*

Lord, please broaden my vision, to see more than what is in front of me.

## Weekend faith Sunday

*James Ch 2 v 14 & v 26 "What good is it, my brothers, if someone says he has faith but does not have works? ...faith by itself, if it does not have works, is dead". (ESV)*

There is no such thing as a living faith that doesn't impact our lives and influence what we spend our time doing. Nothing we could ever do will make us more or less of a Christian. But, every aspect of how we live will be marked by our faith

*In what ways do you think your faith is visible to others?*

*Is there something new that you would like to do,*
*as an expression of faith?*

Lord, please encourage me in the times when it takes bravery to do what you ask me to do.

FAITH

# Chapter 6
# *Hope*

*Psalm 42 v 5 "Why are you downcast, O my soul? Why so disturbed within me? Put your hope in God, for I will yet praise him, my Saviour and my God"*

In secular terms, hope is an optimistic outlook usually relating to something that may happen in the future. A sunny disposition is great, but we tend to feel it when we don't really need it. For many, hope is rolled out and dusted off for special occasions such as Christmas, though this is often a complicated or at least mixed experience for those in caring roles. Then by mid-January, as the last of the decorations comes down hope dwindles, and the reality of real life starts again. But our experience of hope can be different when we recognise that along with faith and love, it is a gift that God gives us, and He wants it to flourish.

David knew about real lasting hope and I love how in this verse he speaks to himself in his distress. He evaluates the state of his soul, not dressing things up or pretending that life is a breeze as we Christians have been known to do. Then he reminds himself of where his hope comes from and he makes a choice to respond to his inner turmoil by praising God. As far as we know, he didn't get a quick fix in his circumstances. But in praising God, I believe that David's hope was restored. When we place our hope in God rather than chance, it opens up a world of possibility. For David, hope returned through praise. At other times, God may direct us to pray, give, encourage, rest, give something up or start something new. God knows exactly what you need to restore your hope. For those in our care, diagnosis and prognosis may or may not change, but having a living hope is a game changer.

Lord, thank You for the gift of hope. Please show me how to respond when my hope needs to be renewed.

HOPE

*Lamentations Ch 3 v 22-23 "Because of the Lord's great love we are not consumed, for his compassions never fail. They are new every morning; great is your faithfulness".*

There is more to the cycles of day and night than astrophysics. New days, weeks and years can bring new hope, but more so if we can lay down that which has gone before. I know that some of us do not always know the joy of uninterrupted sleep, whether through physical or anxious disturbances, but we still benefit from closing a day by laying down more than our physical bodies. The end of the day is the opportunity to lay down that which is not as we would have hoped it to be. Perhaps the day has bought conflicts, and we know that other's words or our reactions haven't been Christlike. Jesus invites us into the safest place of His presence, where we can bring all of that and let His light and love shine into that space. There, we can be completely honest with ourselves and Him. We can come before Jesus and lay down our frustrations, fears and shortcomings and this creates a space to be filled with hope for a new day and for the future. If you have had years of mithering about issues in those moments before sleep, it takes time and intentionality to grow new habits.

When was the last time you stopped and thought about what your hopes for the future are for yourself? Think about the immediate future but then think further ahead. Maybe you could take some time to reflect on that today. Then as you lie down, bring those to God. Also think about those things that you would hope for in your circumstances. If time permits you could extend this to thinking about and then praying for whoever you have caring responsibility for and maybe even one or two others.

> Lord, please remind me to hand everything over to You at the end of each day and let me know Your presence in those moments.

HOPE

*Hebrews Ch 6 v 19 "We have this hope as an anchor for the soul, firm and secure. It enters the inner sanctuary behind the curtain".*

When I was studying to become a Social Worker, we spent a great deal of time exploring what individuals and families need in order to function well. I don't remember much talk about hope, yet we know that those who live in it have far better outcomes in their lives. The hopeful are often able to learn and achieve more, have stronger relationships and even live longer. For those who have experienced many hardships and are left with little or no hope, every aspect of life can be difficult and chaotic.

The writer of Hebrews gives this great image of the anchor of hope keeping us steady. An anchor can keep stable a boat, up to 200 times its own weight. If a person's life represents a small pleasure-yacht destined for calm waters, they may rarely give their small anchor a thought. For care-givers, there are times, if not all the time, when we 'carry' the person we care for and also others around us. If we do eventually get all the needed support services on board, we may feel more like a cruise liner needing a massive anchor to match. We can place our hope in many things around us and some of them may be necessary and great, but they are temporary. When our hope is anchored in God, it is permanent and sure. Though outwardly the storms still rage, we hold on to Jesus like the anchor gripping the seabed. Maybe you need to be reminded today that God has got you and He will keep you steady. When our hope is in God, it takes us into His presence, where heaven touches earth.

> Lord, as a carer I know that I need a big anchor. I pray that my hope will grow to match the size of all that I long for and carry.

HOPE

*2 Corinthians Ch 1 v 20 "For all of God's promises find their "yes" of fulfilment in him. And as his "yes" and our "amen" ascend to God, we bring him glory!" (TPT)*

As a parent, I learnt the hard way to be careful when making promises, because sometimes, I haven't been able to keep them. The issue is that our children seem to forget a lot of what we tell them, but they always remember promises made or broken. I hear myself echoing my own mum's words of "let's just wait and see". But God had no such problem in making promises to His children. There are thousands of promises in the Bible, in both the Old and New Testament. God gives us His word without hesitation. He is for us and with us, and He will accomplish His purposes in us and through us. But not all of God's promises are for right now; and most come about when we participate in the outcome. *Isaiah Ch 40 v 31 ...but they who wait for the Lord shall renew their strength (ESV).* His promises come to pass, out of relationship with Him; His answer to them is always yes, but it may not be just as we imagined or at the time when we expect.

I have never noticed the beauty in this verse in Corinthians before, where our "amen" responds to God's "yes". It happens when we recognise that we can be certain that what He says is true because He is truth. God delights in us as we trust and hope in Him and His promises. We can be thankful for those things that we have seen fulfilled and for when we say 'Amen' (so be it) in faith and hope for those things that are yet to be. We can have a certain hope that one day we, and those we care for, will live in freedom from the pain and restrictions that our minds and bodies experience on earth.

Lord, thank You that You never break a promise. Remind me today of the promises that You have made to me.

HOPE

*Joshua Ch 7 v 10 "The Lord said to Joshua, "Stand up! What are you doing down on your face?"*

Joshua was dejected because his army had suffered defeat. Not long before, he had seen the power of God when, in the previous battle, the walls of Jericho had fallen, giving an unlikely victory to the Israelites. For that battle, God's plan would have seemed comical – to blow trumpets made of rams' horns, then on the seventh day to shout. But Joshua obeyed God and won. But for the next battle, Joshua hadn't consulted God. Instead, he listened to those around him. Joshua also didn't yet know that one of his own men, Achan, had helped himself to the spoils of war that Joshua had specifically warned the Israelites not to touch. Through the Israelites turning their back on God, they bought destruction upon themselves, suffering losses.

Joshua had misplaced his hope and looked for victory through his own endeavours, ending up flat on his face. But God stepped into his hopelessness, telling him to stand up. Joshua needed to put right what had offended God, and he also needed to put God back in the centre of his life. Then God once again came up with the best plan and the Israelites got back on the winning team. Joshua wasn't so unlike us in striving to be self-sufficient and losing sight of the true source of hope. Thankfully, God understands our human condition and still today reaches into our hopelessness. God won't turn us away when we turn back to Him. We all face battles in our caring roles, but God still provides battle plans today, when we ask Him. In fact, He says get up, don't give up. So where are you placing your hope today?

> Lord, thank You for always being there, and thank You too for Your patience as I take a lifetime to learn that Your way is the best way.

HOPE

## Weekend hope Saturday

*Lamentations Ch 3 v 22-23 "...his compassions never fail. They are new every morning; great is your faithfulness".*

Jesus invites us into the safest place of His presence, where we can bring the good, bad and even ugly events of the day. He wants His light and love to shine into that space. There, we can be completely honest with ourselves and Him. We can come before Jesus and lay down our frustrations, fears and shortcomings, making room to be filled with hope for a new day.

*Is there anything that you have held back in your conversation with God?*

*Is there anything that you are feeling consumed by that needs the light of God's great love?*

Lord, thank you for your unchanging love and compassion that never fails. Will you fill me with hope for each new day.

## Weekend hope Sunday

*2 Corinthians Ch 1 v 20 "For all of God's promises find their "yes" of fulfilment in him. And as his "yes" and our "amen" ascend to God, we bring him glory! (TPT)*

There are thousands of promises in the Bible, in both the Old and New Testament. Not all of God's promises are for now; most come about when we participate in the outcome. His answer may not be just as we imagined or at the time when we expect. Take some time to reflect on these two promises today and what they mean for you and the person you care for.

*2 Corinthians 6:18 "I will be a Father to you, and you shall be My sons and daughters", says the LORD Almighty'*

*Proverbs 18:24 "One who has unreliable friends soon comes to ruin, but there is a friend who sticks closer than a brother".*

HOPE

*Romans Ch 15 v 13 "May the God of hope fill you with all joy and peace as you trust in him, so that you may overflow with hope by the power of the Holy Spirit".*

Adoniram Judson Jr was a Baptist missionary in the early 1800s who travelled to Burma with his wife Anne. Sadly, Anne and their three children died serving in Burma, but Adoniram stayed there for almost forty years, founding the first Baptist church in Myanmar. He was a pioneer and the work took many years to establish. In the early years, onlookers would have seen the couple's efforts as hopeless. They tirelessly invested time, energy and love and saw only meagre results. Yet, at the time of his death, there were over 7,000 believers, which later grew to 500,000. Their testimony is incredible and yet nobody would envy the suffering that they endured throughout their lives. Whilst in Burma, Adoniram was imprisoned and horrendously tortured. He could have indulged in some well-deserved self-pity, whilst planning his exit from ministry upon his release. But while in prison, Adoniram's friend sent him a letter and asked, "How's the outlook?" he replied, "The outlook is as bright as the promises of God" (Missionary Biographies).

Anne is also remembered as a stoic missionary in her own right, and I wonder if her husband would have survived prison, if not for her vast capacity to care. During her husband's imprisonment, she moved into a shack close by and cared for not only him but also other prisoners, sending in food and sleeping mats.

Adoniram was a hope carrier and it was not at all dependent on how life was treating him at the time. He had no idea that almost two hundred years later their story would still be inspiring and instilling hope in others. Adoniram and Anne were strong characters, but their efforts alone were not enough to muster hope through each loss and disappointment. Adoniram had started his adult life as an atheist but after encountering the love of God, that love became the driving force for the rest of his life. He kept Jesus at the centre and *"by the power of the Holy Spirit"*, he lived, loved and died in hope.

HOPE

*Romans Ch 4 v 18 "Against all hope, Abraham in hope believed and so became the father of many nations, just as it had been said to him, "So shall your offspring be".*

Abraham and Sarah were already past their prime when God told them that they would become parents. God, not known for 'half measures', pointed out all the stars in the sky beyond what could be counted, telling Abraham that their children would number that many. But another twenty-five years passed before that promise was fulfilled. By now, Sarah was decades past childbearing age, and the couple were under no illusion about the facts of the situation. From verse 19 on it says, *"Without weakening in his faith, he faced the fact that his body was as good as dead – since he was about a hundred years old – and that Sarah's womb was also dead. Yet he did not waver through unbelief regarding the promise of God, but was strengthened in his faith and gave glory to God, being fully persuaded that God had power to do what he had promised".* At different points, both Abraham and Sarah had laughed at the thought of conceiving a child, and Sarah had taken matters into her own hands, leading to Abraham fathering Ishmael with a servant. And yet, through faith, they both came back to hoping and believing that God would do what He said He would do.

Most of us are not strangers to waiting, but when we enter the caring role, it often takes on a new dimension. We wait for appointments, services, tests and results; we wait too in the hope that others will understand. But for Abraham and Sarah, they weren't just waiting, they were longing for the promised child to be born. It might have been tempting for those around them to tell them not to get their hopes up. However, both Abraham and Sarah came to learn that nothing is beyond God's power and that knowledge reshapes the definition of reality. When all seems hopeless, hope finds its purpose. God loves to see our hope in the waiting and in the mystery.

Lord, I thank You for Your promises to me. Please help me and strengthen me in the waiting.

HOPE

*Romans Ch 5 v 5 "And hope does not put us to shame, because God's love has been poured out into our hearts through the Holy Spirit, who has been given to us".*

Not all of our hopes will come to pass this side of heaven, no matter how much faith we have. God spoke to Jacob (Abraham's and Sarah's grandson) about His people inheriting the promised land, but I wonder if he imagined that this promise would not even begin to be realised until Moses came along 400 years later. Then, after leading the Israelites for forty years, Moses didn't enter the promised land either, although God did lead him to a mountain so that he could see it. Yet he is remembered as one of, if not the greatest leaders of Israel. The route to the promised land reflects the Israelites journey to becoming the people God wanted them to be. It was complicated and frustrating. When God showed miracles, the people promised to be faithful, but when life got tough in the desert, they lost hope and became resentful.

In almost every situation I've been in or known about, there is a process between the inspiration or promise and then that becoming a reality. God speaks and then we go through a time of growth and often testing. It is easy to have hope if we don't hang much on it, if we stick with the comfortable, where there are fewer risks. If we never step out, we might avoid some disappointments along the way, but we may also avoid God doing some great things in our lives. Not everything I think I heard God say has come to pass, but in the end, I would rather trust God's leading and leave the outcome to Him. The call to care leaves none of us unchanged, but, if our hope is in God, then we can never be disappointed with the final tally, knowing that we stepped up and lived to honour Him.

Lord, thank You that you care about my hopes, but thank You that you love me so much more.

HOPE

*Proverbs Ch 24 v 14 "Know also that wisdom is like honey for you: If you find it, there is a future hope for you, and your hope will not be cut off".*

It's 2.05 a.m. as I listen to the sounds of wildlife foraging for food; and then my brain connects, and I realise that another anti-snoring device has failed. I refocus on the sound of intense blustery rain. It's been a long winter with much illness, and I shudder at the thought of any more trips to Soft Play. My mind turns to the upcoming week, packed with appointments. Finally, morning comes, and I notice a fence panel is down, exposing a perfect escape route for the children and dog. The trusty shed is leaning, and the rest of the garden looks like footage after a cyclone. The bleary-eyed person staring back at me in the mirror looks like she's lost a fight, with dark circles round the eyes. The children too have been disturbed by the weather, and their day starts with tears and chaos. Nothing terrible has happened; it's just a grey day.

In our climate, it's easy to forget that the sun shines all the time, but we often don't see it because of the cloud. God gives the gift of hope. It isn't a loan to be taken back, but like the sun, it also gets overshadowed. Hope may become obscured by catastrophe, but often it is dimmed just by many small hassles and disappointments. This verse in Proverbs points out that, as we mature, we learn that hope comes from whom we know and applying what we have learnt, rather than just what we feel. I remember playing a game of 'fives' with my children, but it also helps me too, to pause and think of five things I am grateful for and if there is time, five people who have shown me kindness, five times that God has answered prayer etc. It's simple but it lifts me and restores my hope, even on grey days.

What five things could you be grateful for today?

HOPE

*1 Peter Ch 3 v 15 "But in your hearts revere Christ as Lord. Always be prepared to give an answer to everyone who asks you to give the reason for the hope that you have...".*

When we value something or someone above all else, that person or object will usually take pride of place in our home or life. It can be dull being around someone in a new relationship, if they constantly talk about the object of their affections. But as relationships establish and become familiar, it takes effort not to take them for granted. Peter understood that and writes to believers, knowing that it isn't a given that Christ will remain at the centre of our lives as Lord over all. When Jesus has that pride of place in our hearts, we grow and change, and it is impossible for others not to notice. Hope becomes present and noticeable when we consciously, daily, place our lives and circumstances in God's hands. We pray often and become more attuned to His voice.

The majority of us though, I believe, are more distracted than we have ever been before and not just by our daily duties. According to the research company Dscout, the average person touches their mobile phone a staggering 2,617 times each day. If we allowed a good margin for cultural differences or even supposed the study was exaggerated, there is no getting away from the fact that we are addicted to our phones. This is a difficult issue to change, as most of us with caring responsibilities need to be contactable, and so the temptation to scroll is literally at hand. Who would have thought twenty years ago that the God of all creation, who offers us friendship, would be competing with a gadget that is making the world a lonelier place? Perhaps your distractions are not electronic, but let's take some time today to think about who or what has our full attention.

Lord, thank You for the hope that is found in You. Please help me to recognise and overcome all that pushes You aside.

HOPE

## Weekend hope Saturday

*Romans Ch 5 v 5 "And hope does not put us to shame, because God's love has been poured out into our hearts through the Holy Spirit, who has been given to us".*

Not all of our hopes come to pass this side of heaven, no matter how much faith we have. God spoke to Jacob (Abraham's and Sarah's grandson) about His people inheriting the promised land, but I wonder if he imagined that this promise would not even begin to be realised until Moses came along 400 years later.

*Why is hope important, if we can't see any material change?*

*So many people who need care struggle with shame.*
*What difference do Hope and Love make?*

Lord, please help me to grow, so I can say that ultimately my hope is in you, above any thing or situation.

## Weekend hope Sunday

*1 Peter Ch 3 v 15 "But in your hearts revere Christ as Lord. Always be prepared to give an answer to everyone who asks you to give the reason for the hope that you have...".*

Who would have thought twenty years ago that the God of all creation, who offers us friendship, would be competing with gadgets that make the world a lonelier place?

*Do you believe that it is possible to keep Jesus at the centre?*

*Can you think about some of the things that compete for your time?*

Ask God if there is anything that you need to put down, either permanently or for a season?

Lord, I pray that in all circumstances, my hope in you will shine for others to see.

HOPE

# Chapter 7
# *Grace*

*2 Timothy Ch 1 v 9 "He has saved us and called us to a holy life-not because of anything we have done but because of his own purpose and grace. This grace was given us in Christ Jesus before the beginning of time".*

They say that something is as valuable as what someone else is willing to pay for it, so, when God allowed His only Son to be put to death, He showed how much He values us. We need the grace of God to wipe clean the slate of our past and to live a holy life. In giving His life, Jesus was saying 'this is on me', and He literally means all of it. There is no plan B to earn a divine pardon. Grace is, by definition, the unmerited favour of God. I know that I am not always as gracious in my care as I want to be, but each time we bring our failures and weakness to Him, He will help us to grow in grace. We are changed and are being changed by His grace and for His purpose.

Many believers associate grace only with the second half of the Bible, the New Testament, and understandably so. When Jesus came to earth, He brought a New Covenant of grace. But God showed His grace from the start. Back in the Old Testament, He spared Rahab the prostitute, Noah, the Israelites, Jonah, the people of Nineveh – the list goes on. God's plan for humanity has always been grace since "*before the beginning of time*". There is nothing that you have or will ever experience that is bigger than God's grace. But living in it is counterintuitive: we grow up learning that "there's no such thing as a free lunch". And so, we may have the gift of grace, but to live in the freedom of it, we need to fully unwrap it, in both the giving and receiving.

Take a few moments to reflect on what grace means for you and ask God to speak to you over the coming days, as you unwrap it.

Grace

*James Ch 5 v 16 "Therefore confess your sins to each other and pray for each other so that you may be healed. The prayer of a righteous person is powerful and effective".*

As a young person, I thought it was hilarious to hear embarrassing stories of people going forward for prayer in church, not realising that the person they shared all with had forgotten to turn off their microphone! It's one thing to tentatively open life's 'junk cupboard' and let God inside, but confessing to others is a whole new level and one to embark on wisely.

Though healthy plants tend to grow in sunlight, weeds will grow wherever they find an opportunity, and life's weeds thrive in dark, secret places. Our hidden wrongs and hurts can wreak havoc until they are bought out of hiding. When we try to shut things away, they can fester, and truth becomes twisted. Here, James is not speaking about confessing to others our daily minor offences. I believe that this is about the sins that linger, that you just can't seem to shake off. Those vulnerabilities that take hold; or memories of past wrongs done to or by us that keep popping up into the present, taking the mood down a few notches.

Still today, I don't know many people who practise what this verse teaches, and it is a privileged position to be able to hear someone's deep struggles. But when we choose our confidants wisely, and pray for each other, God pours His grace into every situation. It is liberating, it clears out space for healthy regrowth and it brings healing.

> Lord, please show me if there is anything that I need to talk about and pray through with someone else, and teach me more about being that kind of listener.

Grace

*2 Corinthians Ch 3 v 18 "And we all, with unveiled face, beholding the glory of the Lord, are being transformed into the same image from one degree of glory to another. For this comes from the Lord who is the Spirit". (ESV)*

In recent decades, there has been a culture shift towards blame. We can be quick to point the finger yet the fear of being judged drives many of us to find excuses for our own actions. Still, the old hymn Amazing Grace stands the test of time. For almost 250 years, modern and traditional versions have been sung millions of times over. The writer John Newton came to faith whilst he was a slave trader with a harsh reputation. After his dramatic conversion, he came to regret his past, but it took time. When he wrote the hymn, he hadn't fully recognised what horrific suffering his actions had caused. But God changed his heart, and Newton went on to be a prominent influencer in abolishing the slave trade.

Newton's life couldn't be more different from mine and yet we share a connection. We were both lost, then found and changed by the grace of God. Some people seemingly experience instant transformation, and some grow over time, but either way is just as godly and spiritual as the other. No matter what our past has been, who we have hurt or been hurt by, God's grace is still as amazing now as it was for Moses, Noah and John Newton.

In every house I have lived in, there has been a room or cupboard that becomes a dumping ground for everything that at some point needs sorting out. You may be more house-proud, but we do tend to do that with our 'life stuff' too. Yet God also wants to work in those spaces. When we give God the 'Access all Areas' pass, He, by His grace, will do amazing things.

Lord, I give You open access to every space in my life.

# Grace

*Romans Ch 2 v 1 "You, therefore, have no excuse, you who pass judgment on someone else, for at whatever point you judge another, you are condemning yourself, because you who pass judgment do the same things".*

I learnt to drive later than most and so I imagine that in my early driving days other motorists might not have assumed I was new behind the wheel. A day or two after I passed my test, I went around a roundabout and my positioning was a little off. A woman went past and looked furious, smacking her head and miming THINK! It made me smile, and I wondered if, had she known I was a brand-new driver, might she have been a bit more gracious about my causing her to briefly slow down. The truth is, we all make judgements many times throughout the day, mostly based on guesswork. I know that some carers feel others' judgements acutely, especially if the person/s they care for have mental health issues or hidden disability. Aspects of our care may not make sense to others when they only see a small part of a much bigger picture.

At the time that Paul wrote this letter to the church in Rome, there were many similarities to today's society. Rome was diverse, and according to commentaries was "a hotbed of sexual immorality and idol worship". Some were also spiritually arrogant. Paul wasn't saying that we should turn a blind eye and never make judgements about the conduct of others. In fact, it is absolutely right to hold each other accountable, to ask questions if we are not sure if others are struggling and to call out behaviours that dishonour God. But judging other's motives, is 'above our pay grade': it is reserved for God alone. The key message here is that love comes first. Responding in this way always reflects the nature and grace of God. So, before we judge, let's hold that thought, PRAY FIRST AND BE GRACIOUS.

# Grace

*1 Corinthians Ch 15 v 10 "But God's amazing grace has made me who I am! And his grace to me was not fruitless. In fact, I worked harder than all the rest, yet not in my own strength but God's, for his empowering grace is poured out upon me". (TPT)*

When Paul wrote this, he knew more than most about the power of grace. He had been an educated, driven man, likely to succeed at whatever he put his mind to, but he was an unlikely candidate to expand the message of God's love and grace. Up until his conversion, he was dangerous to the followers of Christ, hunting them down and hauling them off to prison. Many who encountered him did not survive. Then Paul was literally blinded (temporarily) by the light of God. Paul was left in no doubt that for every person he had persecuted, he had also persecuted God. But he made an incredible choice in his conversion, not only to leave his old ways behind and become a follower of 'the way', but also in not allowing his past to define him. He declared that *"God's amazing grace has made me who I am"*.

I have heard it said many times "I can forgive but I can't forget". We apply this to others but also to our own failings, and it can become a stumbling block to becoming all that God wants us to be. There are both destructive and empowering ways to remember. Paul never forgot what God had saved him from, but he didn't continually agonise over it either. In letting go of his past, he was empowered by grace. When we encounter God in this way, it releases us from the prison of our past. We have to choose to get up, walk out and move forwards, past each steel bar that represents every hurt and wrong. When we take those steps, we will be empowered to share God's grace with others. It was never meant to be kept to ourselves.

> Lord, thank you for seeing the very best in me. I choose to be defined by your grace rather than my past. Please help me to be gracious towards the one/s I care for, so that they will see more of you.

# Grace

*2 Timothy Ch 1 v 9 "He has saved us and called us to a holy life-not because of anything we have done but because of his own purpose and grace. This grace was given us in Christ Jesus before the beginning of time".*

We are not always as holy or gracious as we would want to be, but each time we bring our failures and weakness to Him, He helps us to grow in grace. We are changed and are being changed by His grace and for His purpose.

*Think back to when you were ten years younger.*
*Are you more or less gracious than then?*

*What have been the influencing factors?*

Lord, help me to stay in Your ways and not wander off into my own ways. Enable me to be more gracious than I am at the moment.

Lord, as we come to the end of these devotions, please help me not to forget the truth of Your love and grace towards me. Help me to let go of all that hinders, and to be the person that You are calling me to be. Help me to love and care for others, in Your strength, as You care for me. Amen.

# Grace

**References**

Matthew Henry Bible Commentary - www.Biblestudytools.com
John Gills exposition of the Bible - www.Biblestudytools.com
Albert Barnes' Notes on the Whole Bible www.studylight.org
www.classic.studylight.org
www.carrollbryant.blogspot.com/2012/09/quotes-by-carroll-bryant-vol-one.html
www.theopedia.com
www.goodreads.com/author/quotes

Chapter 1

www.fairviewpresbyterian.org/blog/2017/7/24/half-truths-god-wont-give-you-more-than-you-can-handle

Chapter 3

Rabbi Alan Lurie Huffpost Updated 03/21/12
www.heysigmund.com/vulnerability-the-key-to-close-relationships
www.goodreads.com

Chapter 4

www1.cbn.com/are-you-fan-or-follower-jesus
www.gty.org/library/articles/A171/dare-to-be-like-daniel

Chapter 6

p34 https://www.wholesomewords.org/missions/giants/biojudson2.html
Judson Quote Accessed Jan 2020

Chapter 7

https://en.wikipedia.org/wiki/Amazing_Grace#John_Newton's_conversion Accessed Feb 20
https://insight.org/resources/Bible/the-pauline-epistles/romans Charles R Swindoll

Accessed Feb 20